theology

cooked

in an

african pot

edited by Klaus Fiedler,
Paul Gundani, Hilary Mijoga

ATISCA BULLETIN no 5/6, 1996/1997, special volume

Reprinted 2000

Published by the
Association of Theological Institutions
in Southern and Central Africa (ATISCA),
P.O. Box 1037, Zomba, Malawi

Special issue of the ATISCA Bulletin, nos. 5 and 6, 1996/1997

Cover illustration: Isaiah Mphande
Layout, cover design and editorial assistance: Celeste M. Geddes

Printed in Malawi by Assemblies of God Press,
P.O. Box 5749, Limbe

theology cooked in

an african pot

edited by Klaus Fiedler,
Paul Gundani, Hilary Mijoga

Contents

Editors' Preface
Theology Cooked in an African Pot

In this book, the first of its kind by the Association of Theological Institutions of Southern and Central Africa (ATISCA),[1] the contributions are at one with Andrew Walls who believes that "an active, working Christian theology is constructed under the Spirit's guidance from pre-Christian materials".[2] These materials or vessels are epitomized by 'pots' which in Africa seem to be ubiquitous in times of happiness or sorrow, in peace or war, at work or leisure, indeed wherever two or three meet for a purpose. The contents of these pots build and consolidate relationships. Little wonder that the Shona people of Zimbabwe say *Ukaana igasva hunozadziswa nekudya* (a relationship is hollow without food).

African pots, before industrialization, were earthen or carved out of wood. In spite of industrialization, these earthen and wooden ware continue to be in use, especially for ritual purposes. They have therefore continued to be valued not as artifacts or antiques but as symbols of the African heritage and have therefore become icons of sacredness. These vessels participate in connecting the living with the living-dead and God. This is why they are made available for use at all sacred occasions in the life of many Africans.

The contributors to this book are making a salutary call to all Africans to avail these vessels in capturing the presence of God in Christ for all Africa. They call African Christians to make these pots the receptacles of the life-giving food that Christ brings to all humanity. This food has to be

---

1 Founded in 1985 under the auspices of the World Council of Churches' Theology Department. Some of the founder members include Dr Ambrose Moyo (now bishop of the Evangelical Lutheran Church of Zimbabwe, Rev Fr Dr J.C. Chakanza, (University of Malawi), Dr H. Ndlovu (University of Swaziland) and Fr C. Mashonganyika (Director, IMBISA; Harare). Prof. John Pobee always acted as the Spirit hovering above the heads of these founding Fathers. These papers are selected proceedings of the Conference held from 9 to 13th December 1996 at Thokoza Conference Centre, Mbabane, Swaziland.

2 A.F. Walls, "Old Athens and New Jerusalem Some Signposts for Christian Scholarship in Early History of Mission Studies", *International Bulletin of Missionary Research*, Vol .21, No. 4, October 1997, p. 153.

stored, preserved, cooked and shared among all African Christians to offer their spiritual gifts to God through Christ in the very same familiar African pots. In their articles, therefore, the authors are not only dealing with the form (pots) but also the content (food) of the Christian faith. The resultant effect is that African faith/spirituality has to take one distinct face in the multifaceted gem that is the Christian religion.

Clearly the 'African pots' here represent the African worldview, traditions, anthropology, and indeed African epistemology which according to these authors, have to form the substratum of the faith and life of the Christians in Africa.

The book consists of three parts: Part I defines the parameters of theology in Africa, while Part II presents and analyses examples or case studies of contextualized theologies in Southern and Central Africa, and Part III consists of contributions by non-African colleagues teaching theology or theology-related subjects in Southern and Central Africa.

Part I

Augustine Musopole, who was the key-note speaker at the Conference, calls for an African wholistic epistemology in theology, able to shatter the fallacies that pit faith against objectivity, church against academy, particularity against universality etc. Such compartmentalization of life and reality into dichotomies gives people a false sense of security, and hence limits their capacity to explore the unknown.

Musopole departs from the Graeco-Western ways of doing theology, based on binary oppositions, and offers a Malawian-based model of doing theology predicated on the concept of *uMunthu*. Such a model, thriving on *nzeru za munthu* (i.e wisdom for humanness), claims Musopole, is a typically African epistemology that connects the human being, not only to God, but to other human beings as well as the whole cosmos. The fruit of the *uMunthu* epistemology is an authentic theology that fulfills the human spirit. To Musopole *uMunthu* offers an interesting *locus theologicus* for all the Bantu people of Africa because of its rootedness in what he calls an 'ontogical cognition'.

B.S. Chuba, a Zambian lecturing in Botswana, discusses the perennial issue that has preoccupied African theologians since the late fifties; i.e.

defining the Africanness of 'African theology'. In his contribution towards this long-drawn debate, Chuba refers to the African socio-economic, political and cultural context, African language, African propagators, and African recipients of the Christian Gospel as important factors in the determination of the identity of 'Africa theology'. Chuba goes further to attempt a blueprint (recipe) for such a theology.

Part II

James Amanze, a Malawian lecturer at the University of Botswana, goes further than the recipe stage; he serves the reader with a theology dish from the Tswana pot. A discerning patron cannot miss the major ingredients that make up the dish. These include faith healing and its relationship to christology in African Initiated Churches (AIC's). He shows how the Tswana, Herero and Kalanga Christians of Botswana have transformed christology by relating Christ to the *modimo* (ancestor) and the *ngaka* (healer) of their traditional past. He, however, shows that these Christians' pneumatology still needs a long way to go before becoming authentically African and at the same time Orthodox. He also briefly discusses the process of contextualizing soteriology and ecclesiology among the same Christian churches. An interesting aspect about this article is the realization that in evolving an authentic theology - as much as in cooking - it takes time and patience to produce the desired product.

Paul H. Gundani from the University of Zimbabwe offers the second case study focussing on the attempts by Catholics in Zimbabwe to produce an authentic African burial rite. This burial rite is an attempt to locate Christ in a more familiar and favourable light and image of the ancestor (Tateguru) of the Shona.

The third case study is provided by Obed Kealotswe, lecturer at the University of Botswana. The article focuses on an attempt by Shadipinge, a *ngaka* (healer) who is simultaneously a Christian, to intergrate Christian doctrine into his ministry of healing. In his attempt to intergrate the mediatory roles and functions of *badimo* (ancestors) and Christ vis-à-vis *Modimo* (God), Shadipinge's exegesis results in a syncretism that the Hambukushu members of the Church of Christ of Shakawe are uncomfortable with. For Kealotswe, however, Shadipinge's theology goes quite far in illustrating the continuities between traditional healing and Christian healing.

In a case stidy from Malawi, J. Chakanza traces the ways in which traditional healers are adjusting to the religious changes brought about by the Christian religion. Like Simon Magus the Samaritan (cf. Acts 8:9-24) and the Sons of Sceva (Acts 19:13-17) the traditional healers studied have made a concerted effort to appropriate new symbols of power through the use of the Christian Bible, and the singing of Christian hymns for the purpose of their healing ministries.

It is important to note, however, that Chakanza's case studies, like Kealotswe's, illustrate the point that African traditional religion is constantly shifting its frontiers by negotiating for space with other religions. Perhaps this is the lesson that Christianity in Africa has to learn as it also fights for space with other religions and philosophies. Such adjustment is an existential imperative if African theology is to be a reality.

The last case study under Part II comes from Ezra Chitando, a lecturer at the University of Zimbabwe. He studies nomenclature as a possible barometer of assessing the extent to which Shona Christians have internalised and continue to identify with the Christian values. Giving names to children, argues Chitambo, has been, and continues to be a vehicle of mediating new knowledge and is therefore a *locus* of theology since the parents are grappling with an existential question about how to be Christian Africans.

Part III

In his articles on how Britain went through the paces of adapting and inculturating Christianity, Bruce Bennett, an expatriate lecturer at the University of Botswana, expresses a sense of *deja vu* regarding much of what has been said about Christian theology in Africa. His advice for African theologians is simple and precise:

> Whoever wishes to climb a mountain top, climbs gradually step by step, and not in one leap.

That piece of advice sounds like it was plucked from the Shona wisdom saying: *Kukwira gomo hupotereka*.

The message is clear to theologians of Africa, not only in the ATISCA region. Cooking theology, as any other kind of cooking, requires discernment and patience. It is not an event but a process. Making it an event may result in the production of rushed and under cooked theology which no one may have delight in consuming. If forced down the throats of the African consumers in the name of Africanization it can only result in necrophilia and not abundant life that Christ promises to his disciples.

Bennett also poses an interesting question for African theologians: Is it the duty of inculturation to reconcile clashing symbols, traditions and worldviews or to secure triumph of Christian orthodoxy over the pagan ideas?

Another expatriate lecturer at the University of Botswana, Saroj Parratt looks at the interaction of the old (Hinduism) and the new (Christianity) among Indian Christians of Bengal, as they tackled the question of the status of women in church and society. She argues for the need of a parallel movement in the church in Botswana and calls for an 'African feminism' that deals with particular cultural problems and needs of the African people. For her the major question that the Christians of Botswana have to tackle is: Who is Christ in situations where men exert their power over women in church and society?

Klaus Fiedler, a 'non-African cook' and expatriate lecturer in the Department of Theology and Religious Studies at Chancellor College, University of Malawi, points to a common African dichotomy between orature and literacy. He calls on theologians in Africa to 'translate' the oral theology that abounds in the African Church into written theology. But then he warns against another African extreme reflected in the tendency to produce elitist theologies which marginalize oral theologies. This results in theologies done locally being transformed and moulded by academic theologians for a Western publisher and constituency. For Fiedler, African theologians have to learn to publish locally in order to give African Christians access to a theology that they have generated. Publishing locally, Fiedler insists, helps build the identity of African churches.

Bon appetit!

Paul H. Gundani

Needed: a Theology Cooked in an African Pot

Augustine C. Musopole

From the moment I came upon the theme of this conference, I have wondered how many African men are familiar with the pots that are found in a kitchen and the use to which they are put. The irony is that in almost all our hotels, it is the men who work in the kitchen as chefs and waiters, but at home, it is the women who are found there. How then can we justify our discussing this theme at a conference dominated by men who know next to nothing about cooking and pots? My humble qualification to speak on this theme is that for almost ten years I was the cook as my wife studied. I know something about pots. My mother was a potter and she made all sorts of pots according to their functions. A pot for relish was different from a pot for *nsima*, or for soaking maize, or for holding drinking water, or for brewing beer. However, they had one thing in common, they were all made of clay. Clay pots are different from metal pots in the way they cook food. The difference lies in their thickness and how they distribute heat once on the fire. Therefore, different pots give the food a unique texture and even taste. On a different level, African pot refers to an African way of cooking and not simply a pot made in Africa. It is this second sense of African pot that provides the imagery and symbolism for our theme.

My subject is the need for a theology that is cooked not in a European or American pot, but rather an African one and more than that a theology that is cooked the African way. Theology in Africa has been cooked in western pots and, therefore, has had a western texture and taste. Our churches have inherited traditional denominational theologies also known as missionary theologies. These are the theologies that underlie the ecclesiastical practices of our churches up until now. They are theological relics with little to do with the realities of today. In reaction to these theologies, several attempts have been made to flavour these theologies with African spices through adaptation, but with little success. The taste proved to be less than African. One could still feel the western taste beneath the African spices. There has been Liberation Theology with its Latin American flavour, but this too has been found to be less tasty largely for being reactionary and western in its methods. A variety of theologies cooked in African pots have been tried with different levels of success. Most of these theologies were cooked following western recipes. What is needed is an African theological recipe and the cooking done in an African pot. This article will attempt to examine the need for a theology cooked in an African pot by providing a recipe.

Before a recipe is given, some clarifications are necessary by way of mental preparation. Mental attitudes are important in the preparation of food if it has to end up being palatable. The discussion that is to prepare our minds will focus on the question of definitions, epistemology, universalism, and cultural considerations.

(A) Definitions

Definitions are contextual and that is why it is important to study words etymologically. In America the word "smart" means intelligent while in Britain it means well dressed. To Aristotle the word *theologia* meant stories about the gods, but that is not what it came to mean to St Augustine to whom it was "faith seeking understanding". What it meant to Augustine is not exactly what it means today. The understanding of theology in Europe today is not the same as the understanding of theology in Africa or in Asia. We cannot take the western view of theology and impose it on Africa without distorting both realities because different historical developments have given a particular understanding to the word and theological phenomenon. Therefore, there is need to define theology in the African context before embarking on its construction. For me, theology is concerned with what I call the with-us-ness of God in the cosmos. This is so because we have a communal view of reality. Nothing is seen in isolation. Everything is related to everything else.

I consider this task of defining our terms as a very important, because some of the foreign terms may not signify exactly in the new context what they signify in the context of their origin. Since the meaning of words conform to the context, a redefining of these words in the light of the context is often necessary. The word theology being foreign to our religio-cultural traditions, it has to be made to signify something slightly different from what it signifies in English. The definitions of theology that were put forward by African theologians tended to be Euro-centric. For instance, Harry

Sawyerr defined *theologia Africana* as based on "sound philosophical discussion". What he had in mind was European philosophy.

We are all familiar with the fact that the word theology is a composite of two Greek words, *theos* and *logos*, meaning word about God. In western theological tradition, theology has been understood as the critical reflection upon God's revelation and understanding. At the heart of critical thought is the principle of non-contradiction resulting in objective knowledge. While such a definition of theology has a place in the cooking of theology in the African pot, its meaning would be greatly curtailed because our central principle is LIFE and not reason. Therefore, I would like to propose a relational definition which takes into account both objective and subjective knowing. Theology has to do with a lived understanding of the with-usness of God in the cosmos.

(B) Universality and particularity

Rationalism does not only insist on objectivity, but also on universality. Just as mathematics is true everywhere, theology, too, must be true everywhere. The more universal, the more abstract, and particularity is dispensed with as too narrow and myopic. Rationalism makes universality and particularity opposites and the result is that we become suspicious of efforts to contextualize theology. Even if we find this acceptable, we tend to seek its legitimization by following western theological methods and retaining western external examiners. According to the epistemology that we are espousing, we can only be universal by being particular. Without the particular there is no universal. Theoretical doctrinal abstraction that seeks to maintain some universal essence without regard for historical particularity, only helps to divorce theological thought from lived experience. Particularity and universality are a continuum and not opposites. The recognition of this fact has liberated us to begin to talk of theologies rather than theology.

(C) Theology and the Churches

It has already been intimated that our churches have maintained relics of missionary theologies most of which have ceased to inform the practice of the Church which has been reduced to mere traditionism. This means that most of our churches are operating without a theological basis. The result is that they are advocating practices that would be hard to justify theologically. Furthermore, it seems to me that either the theology that is taught in theological institutions is not relevant enough or hard to apply that one does not hear it articulated in the pulpits. We are churches without a theology. Three synods of the Church of Central Africa Presbyterian do not have committees on theology, while they have committees on every other conceivable area. While most of our churches have celebrated their centenaries, the word theology is known by very few Christians. I wonder whether the churches will like this theology cooked in an African pot. Many suspect it of being neo-paganism. Unless the churches are convinced about the importance of theology for the life of the church and that theology has to be home-grown, our being here will be a useless exercise in mental gymnastics.

Evangelism and theology belong together and these two are directly related to our *uMunthu*. The church needs to become African in theology and practice for it to be truly African. What is called African Christianity is to a large extent western churches on African soil. Even indigenous churches are not adequately African for being biblical adaptors and adoptionists. It is a truly African theology informing practice which will make African Christianity and church, truly African.

(D) Theology and culture

Even as we seek universalism in theology, we need to remember that theology is always culturally bound. There is no theology which is culture free and this is how things should be. We all come out of a cultural context. Since theology arises out of evangelism and evangelism is about the incarnate Christ, theology takes on an incarnational nature. Much of the theology that we teach in our institutions has little to do with the cultural context of the students. Culture is the pot in which we can cook African theology.

We may use other exotic pots to cook theology, but it will not be African and the church will continue to be theologically malnourished.

(E) Epistemology

Epistemology is about how we know what we know. I contend that while we share a lot about how we know as human beings, different cultures conceive and perceive reality differently in many ways. This being the case, ways of knowing also vary from culture to culture. Since I consider this matter as very important, if we are to come up with a theology cooked in an African pot, the importance of epistemology, theology and especially theology cooked in an African pot, demands that I should make further elaboration.

Christian theology has its roots in the church's witness to Jesus Christ as the Lord who saves humankind from sin and its tragic consequences. In its fundamental and original role, theology is a function of evangelism, and is supposed to have the certainty of salvation/liberation as a living experience for its goal. However, when theology took after the Hellenistic critical spirit, and when in the eighteenth century, with the ascendancy of reason as the final epistemological court of appeal, it conformed to the spirit of the age, theology developed into an end in, and of itself. It became separated from its evangelical[3] basis. The joy of engaging in it came out of the academic interlocking of horns with other disciplines that gave it the greatest challenge, namely, philosophy at first, and science later. Now that list has been added to by the social sciences as competitors.

There would be nothing wrong with theology becoming an end in itself, if this was also the means to its evangelical and salvific end. The problem is that modern western traditional theology has tended to settle for its own legitimation in the academy as its goal and reason for not taking into account the evangelistic task.[2] One reason for the predominance of this tendency is the theological captivity to an epistemology that has failed to come to terms with a basic aspect of the theological enterprise as rooted in the evangelical witness. This basic aspect is the new creation and its concomitant spirituality resulting from a faith commitment, and the role of the Holy Spirit in it. This aspect has been relegated to ecclesiastical concerns and not the academy.

Edward Farley has spoken of the ambiguity of the term "theology" in that it has basically two senses. The first sense sees theology as "an actual, individual cognition of God and things related to God, a cognition which in

---

3 The word "evangelical" is used here in its basic meaning related to the Good News as an existential experience of salvation/liberation brought about by the reality of Jesus in one's life through the agency of the Holy Spirit. It does not refer to systems of evangelical theological thought as such.

2 Confessional theological traditions are no exception. Congress after congress, Evangelicals make theological declarations only to return to business as usual after the congress is over.

most treatments attends faith and has eternal happiness as its final goal". The second sense is one in which theology is "a discipline, a self-conscious scholarly enterprise of understanding".[3] Farley goes on to categorize the former as the habit of the human soul and the latter as a pedagogical discipline. In other words, one has to do with human salvation and its meaning for human existence, while the other concerns the mind, and is focussed on logical coherence and understanding of theological systems.

Farley contends that this ambiguity has not been created by theology, nor by the church, but is an adoption from the encounter of the gospel and general culture in classical times. *Theologia* took on the double meaning of the Greek term, *Episteme*, meaning knowledge on the one hand, and the means to that knowledge on the other. This meaning of *episteme* was in turn taken up in the Latin term *Scientia*. Therefore, theology came to refer to knowledge of God, and to the discipline of study of that presumed knowledge issuing in a body of teachings that could be confessed:

With the rise of universities in Medieval Europe, this second sense became predominant. Farley explains how this came to be the case.

> The result is the appropriation of learning, especially from philosophy, into a framework to explore and express the classical scheme. The result, in other words, is *theologia as scientia* in the distinctive scholastic sense of method of demonstrating conclusions. The distinction between theology as knowledge and theology as discipline becomes sharpened. And as theology as discipline grows in the school, it is also opposed to those who see theology as a salvific knowledge.[4]

In spite of the apparent inner tension, the sense that theological understanding could not divorce itself from the "practical, salvation-oriented (existential-personal) knowledge of God" was reasserted by the Reformation. However, the recovery was to be lost again in Protestant scholasticism that adopted an abstract, analytical, and logical approach of mathematical and physical sciences. Evangelicalism has inherited some of this scholasticism.

Since the Enlightenment the understanding of theology has undergone a radical transformation. Farley clarifies for us what actually happened:

---

3 Edward Farley, "Theologian - The History of a Concept", in Peter Hodgson and Robert King (eds.), *Readings in Christian Theology*, Philadelphia: Fortress, 1985, p. 1.

4 *Ibid.*, p. 4.

> In this period the two genres of theology continue but undergo radical transformation that the original sense of theology as knowledge (wisdom) and as discipline virtually disappeared from theological schools. Theology as a personal quality continues (though not usually under the term *theology*), not as salvation-disposed wisdom, but as the practical know-how necessary to ministerial work.[5]

What emerges is systematic theology, a technical and specialized scholarly undertaking modelled after mathematics and the sciences. Its character is the logical coherence of the system around some arbitrary organizing principle, and not the reality of Jesus in people's lives which was at the centre of New Testament Christianity and which gave rise to Christian theology in the first place. Jesus becomes a theological issue not out of the experience that people have of him (for that belongs to the private domain of their lives), but out of either a concern for a historical figure whose teaching has influenced a large portion of humankind or an attempt to figure out how the divine and the human relate (or do not) in him.

The nature of this restrictive epistemological framework is characterized by a concern for logical coherence and certitude. The models of this epistemological paradigm have been inherited from philosophy (logic), mathematics, and then science, and finally the social sciences. From philosophy, theology has inherited the need for critical, objective (empirical), and coherent knowledge. Hence from this arises the need for propositional rather than incarnational truth. The mathematical aspect which theology has appropriated is based on the certainty of mathematical data and its universal application. These disciplines, that is, philosophy, mathematics and science have influenced theology in the direction of trying to produce logically water-tight systems presented as propositional truths universally applicable. The epistemologies of both Descartes and Kant take after this mathematical paradigm. From the social sciences modern theology has appropriated an ideological character very much in evidence in liberation and political theologies.

From within philosophy, the epistemological constructs of René Descartes (1596-1650), John Locke (1632-1704), David Hume (1711-1776), Immanuel Kant (1724-1804) and the empiricist philosophers have done much to undermine the Christian confidence in talking about certain

---

5 *Ibid.*, p. 7.

experiences which are essential to the understanding of God's activity in the world. The fear of being accused of subjectivism (as if one can have objectivity of thought without the subjective element) caused an epistemological crisis that led to a paralysis of confidence in the faith-salvific knowledge. This is the knowledge of the reality of Jesus made real by the indwelling of the Holy Spirit. In theological knowledge, objectivity is a myth and the fear of subjectivity is a *shibboleth*. Whatever is objective has a subjective element and whatever is subjective has an objective side. Objectivity and subjectivity are two sides of the same coin and are not opposites in the sense that they negate each other, rather, they are complementary. The test of either objectivity and subjectivity in theology does not only depend on logical coherence, but also on the lived life of the person making the theological statements. It is this second aspect in the Christian perception of reality that has been severed in rationalistic approaches to knowledge. Reason cannot be the absolute judge in theology because it is itself not immune from subjective conscious or unconscious distortions in its applications. The very fact that linguistic philosophy, while staking its credibility on relating meaningfulness to verifiability of statements, found that the verifiable principle itself falls victim to its own assertion regarding its meaningfulness, and should make anyone wary of reason's claims and the epistemology based on it to finality.

The derailment of theology from its evangelical salvific-knowledge has largely been due to an imposition of an inadequate epistemological frame of reference, which though better suited to some academic disciplines, has led theology into a dead end by either denying it or making problematic the very elements that made it existentially meaningful. What happened instead is that what was meant to clarify the reality of the subject, restricted it and thereby distorted it. With its roots in the gospel made effective by the Holy Spirit, theology cannot do away with the subjective element, and then expect to hold its own as a discipline only on its objective claims. The failure of the Quest for the Historical Jesus as shown by Albert Schweitzer demonstrates the inadequacy of this approach abundantly. Theology is by its very nature a discipline of the mind as well as of the heart. In other words, it is a reflected witness on our life with God. Its validity is not only in its logical coherence, but much more so a life transformed by the gospel and conforming more and more to the image of Jesus Christ. Therefore, there is need for an epistemology that will take into account the totality of the gospel experience.

Unless theology recaptures the dimension of salvific knowledge as a fundamental aspect to theological apprehension, its value as a Christian enterprise becomes greatly diminished.[6] It faces the danger of becoming the cause of degenerative spirituality in the body of the community of faith. This has been one of the major weaknesses of liberal theologies and may still be for some modern theologies that do not take into account the salvific-knowledge aspect of the Christian experience. The frustration of evangelical theologies stems from the fact that they have uncritically accepted to operate with a restrictive epistemological framework and relegated the discipleship element that has to do with lived experience of the faith to a spirituality divorced from theology itself as spirituality's proper epistemological grounding. Gustavo Gutierrez has strongly reiterated this point. He writes:

> In the early centuries of the church, what we now term as theology was closely linked to the spiritual life. It was essentially a meditation on the Bible geared toward spiritual growth .... The spiritual function of theology, so important in the early centuries and later regarded as parenthetical, constitutes, nevertheless, a permanent dimension of theology.[7]

The current growing interest in spirituality with its own theological grounding as a budding discipline may be ill-conceived because it continues to separate what it should not. We need a theology that is spiritual and a spirituality that is theological because God is spirit.

The approach of Jesus to knowledge and truth may be instructive for the development of an evangelically based epistemology that goes beyond logical coherence of rationalism. Mark 12:18-27 is a discussion on marriage in relation to the resurrection. In the story, the Sadducees set a well crafted, logically coherent trap for Jesus. In response to their question, Jesus tells them that they err because they know neither the Scriptures nor the power of God. It can be deduced from this that the resolution of some theological issues, at least, depend ultimately on both the power of God and an ade-

---

6 The common fear in the churches that theological education destroys faith may not be unfounded and is partly a reaction to a theology made captive by an inadequate epistemology.

7 Gustavo Gutierrez, *A Theology of Liberation*, Maryknoll: Orbis, 1973, pp. 3-4.

quate knowledge of scriptures and not only on logical coherence. This power has to do with the all-purposive wisdom of God. The second incidence that I would like to draw attention to is in John 10:25, 37-38. Jesus points to his Jewish antagonists that if they will not believe his words, then they should at least believe on account of his works so that they may "know and understand" that Jesus is in the Father and the Father in Jesus. Jesus is saying this because, for him, his word was consistent with his works. Word and act validated each other.

These two incidents point to an epistemological principle that needs to be accented in evangelical theology. The principle is: "To know is to do and to do is to know." This is not the case most of the time in our view of valid theology. There is too much word without the work or life to back it, and yet, that is the bottom line of Christian witness. The inconsistency between word and work is perhaps the most obvious sign of the contradiction that sin induces and what undermines any theology. Jesus also taught that the truthfulness or falsity of a prophet is determined not by what they say, but by what they do or how they live. By their fruit are they known (Matt 7:15-23). Here again we see how action is the basic line for the validation of truth. More than all this, Jesus personalizes truth in himself when he declared, "I am the way, and the truth and the life (Jn 14:6)". This underscores concretely what we have been saying, and that is, until theological truth is embodied, owned and acted upon, it is not fully known. Theology as Gustavo Gutierrez reminds us, is critical reflection upon praxis. He reiterates:

> Theology as critical reflection on Christian praxis in the light of the word does not replace the other functions of theology, such as wisdom and rational knowledge; rather it presupposes and needs them. But this is not all. We are not concerned here with a mere juxtaposition. This critical function of theology necessarily leads to redefinition of these other two tasks. Henceforth, wisdom and rational knowledge will more explicitly have ecclesial praxis as their point of departure and their context.[10]

Of the two tasks, namely, wisdom and rational knowledge, I would rather subsume the latter under the former as more in keeping with biblical epistemology and with life choices than simply abstract thought.

---

10 *Ibid.*, pp. 13-14.

The certitude in salvific-knowledge comes from being related in a personal way to Jesus, and it is the Holy Spirit that makes this possible. There is no way in which we can by-pass this experience with its concomitant praxis, and claim theological orthodoxy. The Holy Spirit has an epistemological function as the Spirit of truth (Jn 15:26). The function is that of testifying to Jesus. Effective theological evangelistic outreach depends on this. This work of testimony finds expression in the Holy Spirit's counselling, that is, guiding into all truth (Jn 16:13), and in the conviction of sin, righteousness and judgment. The Holy Spirit reveals us to ourselves by revealing God to us. Without this revelation by the Holy Spirit in the role of convicting, our knowledge of God remains that of God in our own image shaped by human tradition as handed on from generation to generation in distorted shapes. This soon degenerates into a cultural religious ideology called academic theology. In this kind of theology, the Holy Spirit may be mentioned, but is given no epistemological role to shape the thinking and lives of individuals after the likeness of Christ. Theologically, the Holy Spirit is muzzled and quenched and the result is a form of theologizing without its power. This is the kind of theology that the apostle Paul avoided when he said:

> When I came to you, brothers and sisters, I did not come proclaiming the mystery of God to you in lofty words of wisdom. For I decided to know nothing among you except Jesus Christ and him crucified .... My speech and my proclamation were not with plausible words of wisdom, but with a demonstration of the Spirit and of power, so that your faith might rest not on human wisdom but on the power of God (1 Cor 2:1,4 NRSV).

Rationalism left to itself does not know how to handle the reality of the Holy Spirit. Jesus told Nicodemus that as it is the case with the wind so it is with the Holy Spirit. One is made aware of the Holy Spirit, but one does not know where the Holy Spirit comes or goes. We are to be controlled by the Holy Spirit, and not as we do well, control the Holy Spirit theologically. An evangelical epistemology needs to accommodate itself to this reality by rooting theology in the experience of the reality of new life in Jesus made possible by the Holy Spirit. T.F. Torrance in a very comprehensive and highly commendable chapter on "The Epistemological Relevance of the Holy Spirit" says:

> This then is the specific domain of the Spirit in theological knowledge, for by His power and enlightenment we think and speak directly of God in and through the forms of our rational experience and articulation and we do that under the direction of and control of the inner rationality of the divine Being, the eternal *logos* and *eidos* of Godhead.[11]

Without the Holy Spirit there is no revelation to talk about. This is the very Spirit that constituted us into living souls at creation who recreates us after the image of Christ.

Theology needs to be rooted in the doing of the truth as an aspect of the Christian witness to the world. Theology cannot remain a theoretical discipline and claim to be genuinely God-talk that issues in a body of knowledge. This is what distorts the faith by shifting the emphasis from personal trust and obedience to an assent to some propositions logically derived. What is demanded is a commitment to coherent living or living in the truth as the primary task of theological witness. Theological truth is primarily for living and only in a derived way is it for communication in love. Only the Holy Spirit can apply that truth to our hearts and enable us to embody it as a witness to the world. It is this embodied knowledge that manifests the inadequacy of all current epistemological paradigms while at the same time making them serve under it. By restricting ourselves to these paradigms, though useful in some other ways, we rob ourselves of that truth and ability to embody knowledge in mutual ownership which is possible only through the Holy Spirit. The result of opting for restrictive epistemologies is that faith becomes alien and external. One is required to make a "leap" into some dark realm from rationality in order to get to faith. The Christian faith becomes an exercise in irrationality. Faith and reason are considered to be antagonistic. Nothing can be further from the truth.

The basis of theological knowledge is a subjective-objective experience of the reality of Jesus applied to our hearts by the Holy Spirit. It is doubly subjective and objective in that it is an encounter between two beings who embody in themselves subjectivity and objectivity. We need not be aca-

---

11 T.F. Torrance, *God and Rationality*, London: Oxford University Press, 1971, p. 170. I would prefer to speak of wisdom as a more fundamental attribute in God than rationality because God's logic manifests in many respects a different order from our own and can make sense to us only if seen as a manifestation of the divine wisdom.

demically ashamed of making this claim. It is our truth, and we can do no other but to testify to it. Christian truth is apprehended through obedience to the truth as impressed upon one's life by the Holy Spirit. The logical and systematic presentation of this truth, should not hide the need for obedience for fear of being subjective, but to clarify and lead to it as a precondition and goal of faith commitment. When logical coherence becomes an end in itself as demanded by the restrictive rationalistic epistemologies, then theology falls short of its true goal, its incarnational aspect - "And the Word became flesh". Theology as discipline or a body of knowledge is a partial reality and when it claims autonomy it becomes a distortion. Theology understands itself truly when it leads to scholarly discipleship or salvific knowledge. In all this, the Holy Spirit is critical.

In our creeds we confess the Holy Spirit as the giver of life. This fact is very important for an epistemology arising from an African view of reality in the cosmos. The inter-relatedness of reality in the cosmos which I prefer to call ontological or life relationality, is foundational to the personal, communal, historical, and cosmic consciousness of the African peoples. Life relationality is expressed by a holistic way of knowing called ontological or life cognition. Life cognition includes rationality, feelings, faith, doubt, imagination, consciousness, wisdom and all experience. It aims at totality of impression and expression. Life cognition embraces a multiplicity of logical systems which operate relationally in different ways and on different levels. This multiplicity is made meaningful only by our human consciousness in a cultural context. Each individual person becomes a centre of integration and communication of all that experience and the concomitant knowledge.

Preparation of African Theology

The preparation of a meal begins several hours if not days before the actual cooking begins. In Africa, recipes are not often written, but are memorized as they are often passed on from generation to generation. The forethought has to do with ingredients and where to obtain them. When it comes to theology, the ingredients would include: the Bible, theological traditions, African religions and philosophies, life of the church, culture, and history. Let us look at each of these ingredients or theological sources.

(a) The Bible is the primary witness to God in Jesus Christ who has fulfilled and superseded our ancestors, both ontologically and functionary and by incorporating all of us into one salvation history of *uMunthu*.

(b) Having been brought into the salvation history of *uMunthu* in Christ, western theological traditions become an important ingredient if we are going to appreciate the need for cooking theology in an African pot. However, western theology cannot be used wholesale without being treated in order to fit the African pot. There are certain foods that must be treated first, for example by soaking, for them to give a texture preferred by Africans. This has to be done to western theology.

(c) African religions and philosophy provide the bedrock on which a sense of Africanness is established. This is an important ingredient which is meant to give theology that African flavour.

(d) Theology of the living church points to those questions which the Africans are asking concerning the meaning of their relationship with God and the answers that they are getting from their socio-economic and political context in the light of scriptures. The living experience of the church brings theology face to face with various historical situations and thus making it historically accountable.

(e) African culture is the context in which theology must emerge. It is culture that gives theology its particularity.

(f) To be human is to have a history and those significant events that give meaning to one's existence are also theologically significant, because through them and in them God speaks and reveals himself. There is no history in which God is not present. Food does not stop with the gathering of ingredients. It has to be cooked not anyhow, but methodically. The significant question is, what is the African method by which we go about mixing all these in an African pot? If food needs cooking, theology too needs cooking before it can be served.

A Method for Cooking Theology in Malawi

Christian theology is never and has never been monolithic, but rather, it is polylithic and comes into different forms and perspectives. This is as true of the New Testament as it is of the Old Testament. This is a good thing. It is testimony to a God of variety who uses the totality of creation as means of self-revelation. A Chichewa saying goes: "One stone does not build a house nor does one head lift a roof." It takes many stones of different shapes and sizes to build a house. God, the subject of theology (and not its object), is a pervasive God who loves variety and who is pleased to manifest the divine-self in a variety of ways while remaining One. Furthermore, theology and theological traditions are shaped by historical and cultural context, differences in personality and community traits. Therefore, what is being suggested here is one form, possibly of the kind of theology that Rev. Yesaya Zerenji Mwasi, the Presbyterian founder of the Blackman's Church, was calling for, but within the present historical and cultural context of Malawi: A theology that takes "nature, locality, and race" seriously. Rev. Mwasi rejected a universalism in theology that is not rooted in particularity of history and race. Is there a way that could lead us to such a theology for Malawi? I think there is.

Naturally, Christian theology arises out of the encounter that we have with the Gospel of Jesus the Christ, when we accept it as God's way of dealing with our contradictions as it is witnessed to and recommended in proclamation. That encounter happens, when in repentance and by faith, we claim the grace and truth of God for our lives by attaching ourselves to Jesus as Lord and Saviour. The truth of the Gospel becomes intellectually convincing, when by the Holy Spirit, we are persuaded to own up to our sinfulness and are regenerated by the same Spirit. The Gospel is not primarily for intellectual consumption, even though it can be recommended intellectually, but rather, it is for life's commitment. It calls for a trusting personal relationship. God calls us to a life and not simply to comprehend spiritual realities intellectually.

Intellectual comprehension is but one aspect of being alive to God, but it is not the be all and end all. What has happened within the CCAP is that the catechism has become the be all and end all. All one has to do is to repeat from memory the catechism in order to be baptized. The result is professed and not regenerate Christians who are committed to being disciples of Jesus Christ. After a time one is left with communities that have a form of religion, but without the power. It is the illumination of life, and not only the mind, with which theology should be concerned. This is what the gospel of John points us to when it states the mystery of the incarnation: "What has come into being in him was life, and that life was the light of all people. The light shines in the darkness, and the darkness did not overcome it (Jn 1:3-5 NRSV)." Theology has a direct relationship to discipleship because it comes of the churches' witness to a life with Christ. The separation of theology from Christian formation is one of the greatest mistakes of the church. Malawian churches have to reverse this trend before it is too late.

The target of the Gospel as both revelation and redemption is the *Munthu* (human being).[12] Therefore, theology has as much to do with humanity as it has to do with God. Theology is a human activity which is carried out more for the sake of *munthu* (human beings) than of God. It is not surprising then when the gospels say that the sabbath is made for human beings and not human beings for the sabbath (Mk 2:27). God puts the Divine self at the disposal of Banthu. This is grace. It is life. It needs to be remembered that before revelation, there was a relationship, that is, humanity made in the image of God was the subject/object of revelation. It is unfortunate that the word theology is not precise enough in relation to what is actually involved. Karl Barth has suggested theanthropology as a more precise term. It is God in relation, rather than God in the divine essence that we are concerned with in theology. Theology is fundamentally a relational task.

The Gospel targets *Munthu* because *Munthu* is made in God's own image and that means a gracious, life-giving, and blessed relationship with God. It is in God that humanity finds its wholeness, immortality, joy and peace. The Gospel targets *Munthu* because *Munthu*'s integrity has a crucial and critical role in maintaining the cosmic harmony. Harvey Sindima has demonstrated very clearly how this is so. He states:

> The aChewa meaning of creation is life and people are the only meaning discerning creatures .... People and nature form one texture of life. In other words, human life is nature life .... The notion of respect for nature seeks to emphasize the concept of persons as living-in-plenitude, i.e. people have a 'fellow-feeling' with each other and nature .... Consequently people pattern their life to cosmic rhythms. This is based on the understanding that these rhythms stand

12 This is a word found in many Bantu languages in various forms. It is in use from Cameroon all

> for order, harmony and permanence of creation and there is unity between different forms of life.[13]

It is a known fact among Malawians that human actions have either a negative or positive effect on cosmic harmony. With such a cosmic influence, since the Gospel is itself cosmic, it has to target human beings. Furthermore, the Gospel targets *Munthu* because the greatest contradiction in human and cosmic history is centered there. The concept of *uMunthu* underlies this responsibility that *Munthu* carries, which is, to be the priest on behalf of all creation. Here again, Sindima points out that "this relation between human life and the divine mystery, allows people to discern divine intention for human life and the cosmos". However, it is *uMunthu* as related to the Gospel, the Gospel of authentic *uMunthu* as manifested in Christ, that can, I believe, unlock for Malawians a theological understanding that is culturally relevant, evangelically life-giving, and politically, not only challenging, but empowering.

While Rev. Mwasi called for such a theology almost sixty years ago, it is only in the last year or two that the churches have woken up to this theological responsibility. The awakening did not come through the CCAP, but through the Roman Catholic Bishops who in 1992 wrote a Lenten Pastoral Letter in which they courageously pointed out the injustices in the country and called upon the government to rectify them. One hopes that this letter is not going to be a one time reaction, but rather the beginning of theologically wrestling with the realities of life of the people of Malawi so as to establish a sense of meaning and hope. Currently, the Pastoral Letter opened a door for dialogue with the government in which many churches were involved.

Theology and *uMunthu*

It needs to be remembered that the term *theologia* is a Greek word used to describe the cosmic meaning of a Jerusalem happening called the "Christ-event". Theology is not a word that was custom-made for this Gospel-experience. Rather, it was adopted from Hellenistic intellectual culture where it referred to knowledge transmitted through the stories or myths about the

---

the way to South Africa.

gods. Etymologically, means God-talk or word about God. Understood etymologically, the definition of theology has tended to focus largely on God's essential being while the rest of creation and human experience come into consideration only by association and in a derived manner. The kind of theology that this approach fosters is a dry conceptual abstraction, loved by medieval scholasticism and philosophy in every age. It is the natural theology of the worst type. This definition, God-talk, could be an appropriate and adequate one, only if God were an axiom, a mathematical concept, subject only to laws of logic. However, with a dynamic creation that reflects the glory of a Living God and is crowned by a dynamic humanity with whom God is in direct relationship, notwithstanding the Fall, there is a second focus to theology, the *Munthu* in the cosmos. Since God has so chosen to reflect the Godself in the cosmo-related-*Munthu*, it makes *Munthu* theologically significant and part of the definition of what theology is all about. It is the relationship of God to the Cosmo-related-*Munthu* which is fundamentally the content of theology. It is out of this relationship that God can be personally known and through which human beings also can come into their own.

God's revelation is to, for, and with *Munthu* and as such it depends on the response of *Munthu* for its efficacy. This is not to make God depend on humanity, but to make humanity also a proper subject/object of God's revelation from the start. Without humanity, God would still be God, and the divine revelation would still be possible, but there would be no humanity to respond to it and, therefore, no theology. Speculation aside, it is rather for the sake of humanity that revelation is given both in nature, culture, history and in Scripture. Understood evangelically (not simply metaphysically or philosophically), it follows that within the Bantu context of Malawi, theology can only be a reflection on the WITH-US-NESS-OF-GOD. The aim of such a reflection is the embodiment of *uMunthu* as seen in the face of Christ in fulfillment of our creation design and priestly role in the cosmic temple on behalf of the rest of creation. Theology is not simply God-talk, but rather as Herzog has put it, God-Walk, but more precisely, God-Human-Walk. This is what the incarnation is all about. The incarnation is God theologizing concretely. So theology is talking about our God-human-walk, that is, the God-with-us-ness in the entire cosmos. Sindima talks about bondedness. He writes:

> Among the aChewa and in Malawi as a whole, basic values are symbolized by *moyo* (life) and *uMunthu* (personhood). These symbols are foundational in the understanding of life and the world .... *Moyo* is an all encompassing and overarching symbol of living. It forms the basic framework of interpretation in Malawian society. This because it speaks of what creation is for and what it is intended to achieve. Creation is intended to be home of life and its aim is to serve life as life breaks frontiers and reaches superabundance. The first meaning of *moyo* has to do with the cosmos. *Moyo* refers to cosmological ordering since it inhabits life. This means that creation is understood as life .... The idea underlying the concept of bondedness is rooted in the symbol *moyo*.[15]

If humanity is at the centre of creation spirituality or vitality, then God is the over-arching reality embracing the whole creation. Indeed, this follows logically from what Sindima has already said about life. He identifies *moyo* with God, because God is LIFE itself.[16]

It needs to be said from the outset that to emphasize the togetherness of God and humanity is not to belittle God or even to attempt to make God after the human image. God forbid! It is, rather, to assert that out of this felt-kinship-relationship with God, humanity recognizes God's greatness or all sufficiency. It is out of this relationship that we gain the knowledge of God as both transcendent in his immanence and immanent in his transcendence to the point of even dying that the diviners might be revealed as capable of meeting the totality of human experience. Malawians do not conceive of immanence and transcendence in God as opposites, nor do they hold them in tension, rather, they are taken as two sides of the same reality. They are complementary attributes that can be adequately understood only in terms of each other in the reality they qualify. Without this felt-kinship-relationship (immanence), there would be no way of knowing personally the transcendence of God and God's overarching presence. The God who is with us (*Mulungu Nafe*) is at the same time the Most High God (*Mulungu-wa-Mwambamwamba*).

---

15 *Ibid.*, p. 14.

16 "It was indicated above that according to the aChewa thought, all life has its origin in God. Furthermore, it was mentioned that the aChewa maintain that the giver of life, the Divine mystery, is LIFE itself (*Ibid.*, p. 14).

To have no felt-kinship-relationship with God in Christ through the regenerating power of the Holy Spirit, God would remain a very distant deity or only a philosophical concept, logically deduced and very fuzzy. Unfortunately, this is the way God often has been treated. On the contrary, God is with humanity from the time of creation and it is out of this relationship that God acts specifically in history. The Biblical understanding of history presupposes this relationship. It is not the covenant that constitutes human beings into God's image, but God's image leads to covenantal relationship. It is not the seemingly special acts that establish God's relationship with the world. God does not intervene in history as an outsider. Whatever is referred to as God's intervention only presupposes and confirms the already-presence of God, God's permanent involvement and relationship with the world. God does not need to intervene in history because God is always involved with history, redirecting humanity from its own folly in the perennial struggle of life and death.

The reason we view God as an outsider, who must intervene from time to time, is that we have surrendered nature or creation to a false autonomy, that is, treating nature as if it were the be all and end all. Ultimacy is given to that which is not ultimate and God is restricted to the supernatural. The result is a struggle between naturalism and supernaturalism. From a Malawian understanding, I refuse to allow such a dichotomy. It distorts the reality of God on the one hand, and of humanity and nature on the other. This is a false struggle. It is the creation of our wrong headed intellectualism and the result of a Cartesian bifurcation of nature. The truly natural is what is under, in and with God. God is the most Natural Being there is. To be with, in, and under God is the most natural thing human beings can aspire to, while to be with humanity is the most natural things that God does.

God's purpose in history is constant, and that is, to love humanity into fullness of life and freedom as at creation. It is to have a relationship with humanity that even death cannot dissolve. However, the question of humanity's attitude toward God is a different matter. While the With-Us-Ness of God does not historically begin with the Bible, the Bible affirms for us that it goes back to the beginning of creation. The Bible and many myths of creation bear testimony to this fact. Since creation, God has not left humanity alone, sin not withstanding. The story of Cain confirms this view. Neither does God's punishment inflicted on humanity as a result of sin negate it, but rather confirms the fact of God's loving concern and involvement in history. God's spirit struggles with human spirit for humanity's sake. As long as humanity continues to be, God's loving struggle for human authenticity, liberation, and abundant life will continue. Therefore, theology has to do with the relationship that we have with God and has to be approached from the perspective of *uMunthu* as encountered in Jesus. Theology is primarily a matter of living the truth under the direction of the Holy Spirit, the Spirit of truth.

Umunthu, Theology, and Gospel

It is now clear why I have privileged *Munthu* as a theological subject, not in terms of traditional Christian anthropology, but rather in the very definition of what theology is. I want to make it very clear here that the term *Munthu* is understood as encountered in Christ, and not of humanity after the Fall. It is what Paul calls the new humanity. I would now like to elaborate more on what Malawians understand by the terms *munthu* and *uMunthu*.

For analytical purposes only, there are five related aspects to humanity that are significant in the understanding the one reality of *uMunthu* in Malawi. These are: form (*thupi*), spirit (*mzimu*), community (*mudzi*), integrity (*chilungamo* or *kukhala owona mtima*), and (economic) productivity (*ntchito*). All these aspects or dimensions of our being were mandated at creation and define *uMunthu* (humanness). While form, spiritness and community are naturally given or innate, integrity and productivity are capacities that are meant to develop with *maleledwe* (social-nurture). Nurture is a process of *kukula mu uMunthu* (humanization). The first three precondition the last two. The form or body is our individuation, the spirit is our capacity for relationships, while the community is the social arena for our growth and responsibility. A demonstrable embodiment of the last two is necessary in an acceptable view of *uMunthu*, otherwise, one runs the danger of degenerating into a "beast with a human face". *uMunthu* is the essence of human character manifested in and through these relational and survival dimensions of our existence. Relational dimensions serve to connect the human being to other forms of being, and survival ones are there to maintain and sustain life. On the relation of life and *uMunthu*, Sindima states:

> We have seen that *moyo* is an all-pervasive symbol of interpretation. But this symbol can remain an abstraction if not grounded. ACHE thought maintains that what people seek in their work and life is fullness of life itself. Therefore, to ground the symbol of *moyo*, the question of fullness must be addressed. For the ACHE, fullness is in realizing *uMunthu* (personhood) *uMunthu* symbolizes all that is good and worthy in human life or a historization of *moyo*. In other words, *uMunthu* stands for all basic values of human life, or that which gives life meaning.[17]

The reality of *uMunthu* as embodied in the *munthu* has an external as well as an internal dimension. While the external aspect is defined by form or body, the internal aspect is defined by character or spirituality. It is through relationships that one touches on and comes to know the reality of these aspects of existence.

Spiritness, what Sindima has referred to as *moyo*, links human beings to *naMalenga* (a feminine attribute meaning Creator) who is Spirit itself. It is out of this aspect that human beings can be said to be made in the image of God. *uMunthu* is total human integrity which is crucial to cosmic interrelatedness, harmony and salvation. With such a responsibility, it is impossible for humanity to carry it out alone, but only in fellowship with God and the support of the rest of creation. To have moral integrity and to be responsible is to participate in the character, therefore, life of God and thus to become a channel of abundant life to the whole creation. To be *Munthu* is to be a spiritual being.

Form gives us our physical shape and identity. It has to do with our individuation. It links us to the material world from which part of us came, according to the Bible and other myths of creation. Form relates humanity to space and gives it a sense of geographical and historical rootedness.

Community has to do with our relationship to other human beings. It is in community that our *uMunthu* is actualized as an inseparable and yet individuated *Munthu*. Therefore, human identity has a communal dimension. Mbiti has stated it very appropriately, "I am because we are, and since we are, therefore I am". Human beings do not live in a vacuum and

---

[17] *Ibid.*, p. 14.

they do not live on nothing. They are surrounded by a whole varied world of living and non-living things upon which they depend for their physical and social existence. Theirs is a dynamic, but differentiated environment created and maintained by God for their well being. There is a relationship that obtains and is characterized by love/fear, a desire to know and be known or to control. Hence there is an impulse to live circumspectly in order to avoid that which is harmful and maximize that which is good. To be *Munthu* is to be a social and political being.

No matter how human beings respond to the totality of their universe, there is a spiritual relationship which is fundamental to this response. This is what religion is all about, human beings trying to bond with or finding themselves in other subjects or objects. Any such state of relating, (positive or negative) or being bonded, is a religious one. The most authentic bond or relationship is that between God and human beings. To be made in the image of God is to be intrinsically religious and intimately bonded. This means that to live as *Munthu* is to be a walking religion.

Integrity or *uMunthu* has to do with what we consider and make ourselves to be as manifested in our thoughts and actions. It is the inner counterpart to the form. It means being true to ourselves and others. Only other people can testify to that. Without this sense of integrity in life and relationships, our humanity gets compromised and one's life, community and world is adversely affected. To be *Munthu* is to be a responsible being.

Productivity, refers to the enrichment of one's life and that of the community through work. Whether through economic, biological, social and educational undertakings, it is a valued index of assessing the essential *uMunthu* of someone. To be unproductive is to refuse to be human because it is not to care about personal or communal life. It is to abdicate responsibility. This is why laziness or slothfulness is a sin. To be a human parasite is to feed on the life of others. Only witches and minors do that. A person who has *uMunthu* strives not only to feed him/herself, but in the process of feeding him/herself, he/she feeds the community as well. For the wellbeing of the community, this concern for one's own well being and that of the community has to be mutual. They are complementary concerns. To be *Munthu* is to be an economic being.

Traditionally, Malawians have put the high premium on the cultivation of *uMunthu* as a way of being in the world and this outlook has informed the liberation struggle against domination, racism and exploitation. However, it has been lost sight of as we have given in more and more to material oriented economic and political policies that have not always taken *uMunthu* very seriously. There is always the danger that making money, structures, ideologies and institutions become the goal of these policies instead of making them to serve the promotion of *uMunthu*.

While the perspective of *uMunthu* is basic to the culture and religion of Malawi, Christian theology must insist that it is *uMunthu* as manifested in Jesus that has to become the theological norm for Malawi. Ours is a Christo-*Munthu*(ist) perspective. It is human integrity as seen in the face of Jesus Christ. It is out of this perspective that we can speak of the with-usness of God.

What is the Gospel?

Writing a couple of decades or so after the exaltation of Jesus, Mark begins his gospel with these words: "The beginning of the Gospel about (or of) Jesus Christ, the Son of God (Mk 1:1). That word "beginning" is not simply applicable to the story of John the Baptist or even the first preaching of Jesus, but rather to the whole story that Mark was going to narrate. The whole sixteen chapters of it comprise the beginning of the Gospel. The main protagonist is Jesus, *Mwana-waMunthu* (Child of the Human One). Therefore, the Good News is none other than Jesus the Christ, the Son of God. This one whom Mark calls the "Son of God" preferred to call himself "Son of the Man", in other words, *Munthu*. A combination of these two descriptions: Son of God and *Munthu* points to God-with-Us.

A question might be asked, what is good about the news concerning Jesus? For whom is it the Good News? The story that Mark presents is one of good news for those who heard him, who were healed, taught, and fed by him, who saw his mighty works, experienced his forgiving grace and acceptance, and lived to witness the Easter story. It was good news to the poor, the captives, and the blind. It was open good news to the rich, if they were willing to meet its demands. Jesus confronted the forces of destruction, contradiction, and death and routed them. He understood his mission as one of "preaching the good news to the poor, proclaiming freedom for the prisoners, recovery of sight for the blind, to release the oppressed and to announce the year of the Lord's favour (Lk 4:18f)." He preached the message of the Realm of God that challenged all political arrangements with a totally revolutionary way of life. Jesus was indeed Saviour par excellence.

Those whom he restored to health by healing their diseases and forgiving their sins felt fully Banthu again. Jesus was seen to be the one who restores *uMunthu* or life. He was the authentic Sing'anga (healer). Death comes in many forms, shapes and sizes. It is sometimes slow, sometimes fast, but always sure of its prey. And when one finds a healer who can deal with it in all its manifestations, then it is great cause for celebration. Jesus is one who has been through death and yet came out victorious. Death does not have the last word, but Jesus does. The writer to the Hebrews has stated that by overcoming death, Jesus has released from the fear of death those who were held under its power. As a result, he has become the author of eternal salvation based on his indestructible life (Heb 3:14,15; 5:9; 7:16). This fact comes as good news to any and every human being. Gospel is the news of security from the forces and all forms of death, that is, anything that undermines life or *uMunthu*. Jesus is such a one that those who put their trust in him for their lives of *uMunthu*, find him to be not only the perfect *Munthu*, but one who is able to help others realize their own.

This is why St Paul, who opposed Jesus by persecuting the church, was once able to say after turning his life over to Jesus, "I am not ashamed of the Gospel, because it is the power of God for salvation (liberation) of everyone who believes (Rom 1:46). Mawelera Tembo, the first Ngoni Christian in Malawi and a song writer says, "Jesus calls to the sinners to cause them to become righteous".[18] And there is another hymn that summons the soul to jump, dance, celebrate and to be at ease over God's salvation.[19] And there is another song that refers to a yoke that has been removed by Jesus.

Ndawakwanga ndapona,	*I a sinner have been saved,*
goliwoli lasutuka,	*the yoke has been removed,*
Landifyenyanga m'singo 'mo,	*it was suffocating me*
Yesu wakandiwombola.	*and it is Jesus who has saved me.*

---

[18] Hymn no. 245, verse 5. "*Wakucema Bakwananga (repeat) Bazgoke bakunyoroka*", in *Sumu za Ukristu*, Blantyre: Hetherwick Press, 1983, p. 147.

[19] *Ibid.*, hymn no. 260.

Ndasutuka, ndawombokwa,
Yesu wakhara mkati 'mo,
Wakuya nane m'Zioni,
Batuba ba kuhenera.

I have been released, redeemed,
Jesus lives in my life,
and he is taking me to Zion
and the angels are jubilant.

Vikondo vya murwani 'mwe
pafupi kundimarizga.
Ndamwene na nyumba yane,
Yesu wakandiwombola.

The burdens of the enemy
nearly killed me.
Me and my house,
it is Jesus who has saved me.

All this is the testimony of Malawians to the Good News of Jesus. Unless people can experience for themselves the power of the Gospel of Jesus, the authentic *munthu*, in their own lives, they will not be able to know the depth and totality of liberation that Jesus brings from powers and principalities, visible and invisible. It is where people feel to be less than Banthu because of the oppression of sin and evil, in its personal and structural forms, that Jesus begins to apply his liberating power. It is only when we discover that the inner alienation is directly related to the oppressive structural and institutional forms, that we can appreciate the fact that the forgiving of our sins by Jesus, cannot be divorced from the removal of socio-economic injustices as demanded by the Reign of God. And that the demand for justice is a call for all concerned to repent. Jesus is not just a good example to follow or the personification of an ideology, but a real and authentic Saviour of real people, who is as real today in transforming lives and society as he was then. It is as a revolutionary saviour/liberator that Jesus is the Good News. His revolution begins with individual lives and it is these that carry on the socio-political and economic revolution. They are the salt of the earth and the light of the world. It is impossible to have one without the other, and to separate them is to divorce what God has joined together. And yet, this is exactly what the Church has done on many fronts, causing a lot of theological confusion. The salvation that Jesus brings is total and is aimed at the total liberation of the total persons. This is why it is the Good News. If it were not for the reality of this personal encounter with the risen and exalted Jesus through the regenerating agency of the Holy Spirit, Christianity could remain only an ideology like the thought of Mao. By making Christianity only an intellectual enterprise for the theological club, we run the danger of turning it into an ideology without life and power to transform people from within.

One of the public acts that Jesus does in the gospel of Mark is to call disciples. This is the kind of relationship Jesus wants to have with each person. He wants to make people like himself. He invites them to learn to live his kind of *uMunthu*. Learning to live his *uMunthu* is the liberating responsibility to which disciples are called. The tragedy in our churches is that the churches as institutions have come between Jesus and the people. Jesus is known by members mostly as part of the church tradition. He is a glorified patron saint. The result is that churches are full of members, but not disciples.

Jesus demands an immediate relationship with us. Not even the Church, let alone the pastor or priest, or doctrine can dare come between as a mediator. That is the role of the Holy Spirit. Jesus invites each person to be individually yoked to him and to learn from him (Matt 11:29). Unless I know Jesus to be the Good News for me, I do not know him and I cannot become an effective witness for him. Church membership can be made fully meaningful only in the context of discipleship. This does not mean that subjective experience becomes the norm, but rather that Jesus who is the norm authenticates the experience by becoming real. After all, we are not called to prove Jesus objectively, but to bear witness to him from within the community of faith. It is the Holy Spirit's work to authenticate Jesus to those who dare taste him to see if he is indeed good.

There are many who mention the name of Jesus, but who do not know him existentially in a pragmatic and personal way. They are confused about his identity like those who thought Jesus was one of the old prophets. The trouble is that even those who claim personal knowledge (as is the case with many born-agains), tend to turn that knowledge into a religious ideology to arrogantly beat other people with it, contrary to the merciful teacher who will not break a bruised reed or quench a smoldering wick until the full *uMunthu* comes into fruition (cf. Isa 42:3). Those who know Jesus personally as Saviour and Lord are called to a faithful and credible witness and not to spiritual arrogance.

Jesus is the Gospel because he saves me from becoming a beast with a human face and makes me a *munthu* (child of God) who truly reflects the glory of God, as one remade in God's image and likeness. Jesus is good news because he announces the Reign of God which challenges our unjust societal structures and institutions, while introducing a transforming presence. Just as individuals are called to be Christlike, so also the Church, the primary of all institutions, is meant to be like the Reign of God. The reformed principle, *Reformanda semper reformata* (reformed and keeping on reforming) applies to both the individual and the institution if the Reign of God is to be made real and "visible", not only in Malawi, but in the world.

Umunthu and Gospel

Even though I have talked about *uMunthu* and the Gospel in a way that their relationship is apparent, I would like to draw into focus that relationship. How is *Munthu* and *uMunthu* evangelically relevant? *Munthu* is created with divine dimensions by being created in God's image. To be in God's image is to be endowed with the capacity to relate to and even participate in God's being and for God to do the same. *uMunthu*, as manifested in Jesus, is the ability or capacity to relate to God, to be in communion with God. It is by the manifestation of *uMunthu* that human beings truly define themselves as *homo religiosi*. It is our historical spirituality.

If it is by *uMunthu* that we define ourselves as *homo religiosi*, then, it is necessary to redefine our view of religion. According to this view, religion does not mean a system of beliefs, nor ritual practices, but rather, who we are as we live in relation to other beings and to God. Beliefs and rituals are secondary. Beliefs and rituals are not the raw materials of religion. Relationships are the basic matter of religion. Therefore, since religion is being who we are, there can be no atheists or secularized persons in Malawi. Either one practices good religion or bad religion by the way they live and manifest *uMunthu* in their lives. Either one *ndi Munthu* (is a human) or *si Munthu* (is not human). Whatever diminishes or prevents the full manifestation of *uMunthu*, which is supposed to coincide with the will of God amounts to the bad practice of religion and the Bible calls this *tchimo* (sin). Whatever makes *uMunthu* to shine forth is the good practice of religion and the Bible calls this *chilungamo* (righteousness). It is to be aligned with our essence, that which the community knows to be good and is in accordance with the will of God.

Due to sin, our *uMunthu* is not only questionable, but inauthentic. To be authentically *Munthu* is the same as having the image of God restored on the path to its original splendour. To be in God's image is to be open to communication from God and through obedience to be one with God through Jesus the Christ. The faith encounter with the spirit of Christ points one to the reality of this authentic humanity by a spiritual experience that highlights negatively human sinfulness, or beastliness, or the inauthenticity of *uMunthu*; and positively, the glory of God or God's holiness, and authentic *uMunthu* in the sense of human integrity.

Secondly, *uMunthu* is evangelically relevant because of the incarnation, the divine spirit's embodiment of matter. The first incarnation happened at creation when God breathed his breath in that clay form and as a result of which it became a living soul, that is *Munthu*. We are incarnational beings by creation and, therefore, we live by the vitality of God's breath or spirit, individuated as *Munthu*. Our God is the God of life. The incarnation of Jesus is a re-enactment of our creation, hence it constitutes the possibility of our own recreation and a concrete reminder of our life-kinship to God. It is a recapitulation of our origins and the glory that was given to us by God so beautifully captured by the Psalmist:

> What is *Munthu* that you are mindful of *Munthu?* the *Mwana wa Munthu* (the child of the Human One) that you care for him/her? You made *Munthu* a little lower than the heavenly beings and crowned *Munthu* with glory and honour (Ps 8:4,5).

The writer to the Hebrews saw in this passage none other than Jesus, the authentic *Munthu*.

It is when a sharp dichotomy is made between God and humanity, spirit and matter, grace and nature, faith and reason, the natural and the supernatural, that incarnation becomes problematic. There is a creational reciprocity between all these and Malawians do not make that sharp distinction. They know that matter is interpenetrated with spiritual reality. The Spirit does not abhor matter because Spirit [or Word] is the creative force in nature (Gen 2:2). It is when we stick with Hellenistic conceptions in which divinity lives in abhorrence of matter that we find it difficult to relate the divine to matter. The God as divine is capable of interpenetrating matter, even sinful matter at that, because God is divine. If God could not do this, then God would be less than divine. Being divine is not an obstacle to relating to matter, but is the capacity to do so. The fact that divinity is capable of taking on matter should not lead us to thinking that divinity can only be known in material terms. Divinity is essentially spiritual. While matter is capable of accommodating spirit, it is not spiritual in itself. Hence the need for it to be transformed according to Paul (1 Cor 15:50-52). Since incarnation is the historicalization of our existence, it does not negate our spiritual capacity, but rather establishes it.

Thirdly, *uMunthu* is further relevant to the evangelical witness because it is where the problem is located that has committed the whole creation to futility (Gen 3:7; Rom 7:19-21). The saying, "*kulakwa nkwamunthu*" meaning "to err is human" betrays this tragic sense of our humanity, a sense that deforms the reality of *uMunthu* as God intended it. It is a sense that leaves nobody exempt and thus confirming the fact that, left to ourselves, *uMunthu* is an ideal that the socialization process tries to achieve, as cultural salvation, but continues to fall far short of it. In Jesus we can go beyond cultural salvation.

Lastly, but not least, *uMunthu* is evangelically relevant because it is biblically significant. St Paul speaks in contrasting terms of "the first man" and "the second man"; "the man of the earth" and "the man from heaven" (1 Cor 15:44-49).

The writer to Timothy describes Jesus as "the man" (1 Tim 2:5). We have already alluded above to Jesus calling himself "Son of Man". In Jesus our humanity is recapitulated so that it is in line with the divine image in which we have been created. It is no longer the opposite of divinity, but the receptacle of the divine life. God is at home being in humanity just as humanity is at home being in God. This is the reconciliation that Paul talks about to the Corinthian church and of which we become ambassadors (2 Cor 5:16-21).

It is in the *uMunthu* of Jesus that we experience our authenticity, the historical realization of our real nature in and under God. How do we know it is our authentic nature? We know it because, in our encounter with the reality of Jesus by the agency of the Holy Spirit, we encounter God and ourselves. It is a transparent humanity through which the glory of God is refracted so that we see at once a *Munthu* and God our *uMunthu* and Divinity. However, when we look at ourselves, like Isaiah, our response is, "Woe is me, for I am undone!" As God redeems us for the divine self, we experience God being authentically with us. It is this that leads to authentic God-Human-talk as a personal human experience leading to existential and historical knowledge. This is the knowledge of Jesus which is finally unmediated by the church, or even theology, but instead, which establishes the church, that is, the community of *uMunthu* and the truth by which it lives. Like the people of Sycar, one is able to say, "I no longer believe just because of what you said, now I have heard for myself, and I know that this *Munthu* is really the saviour of the world (Jn 4:42). It is this experience of the Gospel that leads to a theology that is incarnational by taking nature, locality and race seriously because the Gospel is the living force that places these in their proper perspectives.

Umunthu and Wisdom

Different cultures emphasize different aspects of knowing and conceiving reality. Whatever tends to receive the greatest attention and emphasis by the way it captivates people's imaginations, dominates a particular world view as the controlling epistemological perspective. It is such dominant emphases which give the epistemological systems their distinctiveness while at the same time either validating or invalidating the other cultural and historical emphasis and systems. It so happens sometimes, for reasons that are not epistemological, that some systems will claim universality of application and dominance in the epistemological arena to the point that other emphases are silenced or marginalized.

This has been the case with western epistemological systems, especially, critical and scientific rationalism. Rationalism has been championed since the days of Socrates, reaching its heyday in the Enlightenment as the be all and end all of all ways of knowing. Nothing could be seen as true and scientific knowledge that did not fit into Kant's four categories or could not survive the Cartesian doubt. Of course, for us in Malawi, this attitude was aggravated by a Eurocentric cultural-political mind set which resulted in the self-aggrandizement of Europeans, the cultural, political and economic conquest of non-European peoples all over the world. Even though this critical and scientific rationalism, either as a philosophical position or as a scientific method, has proved very fruitful in terms of physical research, technological development and the understanding of the material created order, it proved disastrous for people of colour.

Malawi, like the rest of the colonized countries became both a beneficiary and victim of this Eurocentric mind-set. It seems strange to speak of benefits accruing from an oppressive culture and people. However, there are some ways of being and doing which prove good, useful and vital for human survival. The gospel is indeed a plus for Africa, even though the cultural and historical form in which it came left a bitter taste and much to be desired. The scientific approach and the resulting technology is another benefit, its evils notwithstanding.

The traditional educational systems which were to a large extent life affirming, communally based and guided by the educational principle of *nzeru* or *mahara* (wisdom) came under attack as pagan or was paid no attention to at all. It was ridiculed into humiliation. And yet, a communal life, guided by wisdom, was meant to result in a good community. This good communal living was constituted and maintained by all vital aspects of *uMunthu*. However, since the colonies were meant to service the needs of the colonial powers, it was their kind of education based on the accumulation and reproduction of facts and aimed at servicing the capitalist needs; a system divorced from the way people lived their lives, was imposed on Malawians. Good living became simply an aspect of an education dubbed as moral education, and not the basis of it, enforced by the whip, the only tool deemed effective in making the African learn the new ways.

As a method of control, the critical and scientific aspects were not imparted only when they served the capitalist ends, lest the indigenous people became like the colonizers and turn these epistemological tools against the colonial rulers. Libraries were purged of any literature that could be used against the colonial power. The result was that most of the critical and politically revolutionary literature and ideas had to be either smuggled into the country or passed on by word of mouth by those who travelled to other countries, especially South Africa, for further education. This meant that western revolutionary ideas spread out slowly. It was the involvement of African soldiers in the two world wars that brought about the rapid dissemination of political ideas which when brought together with the local spirit of resistance, ignited the fire that consumed colonialism.

The minimum western education that Malawi inherited from Britain, the colonial power, through the agency of Christian missions, dominated effectively the impact of traditional education and established a tradition of intellectual dependence on the West. To be educated was to have imbibed as much as possible a western type education. This system of education used the vernacular only as a springboard for reading. By the third year, English was introduced and everything was to be done in English. With English, a whole new world and way was introduced, leaving the student a victim of intellectual schizophrenia and a child of two worlds. The traditional focus on wisdom was overshadowed. In order for our thinking to be valid, it had to conform to Western standards. The African ways stood like a captive before the Supreme Court of European Enlightenment and constantly found guilty of not living up to the European standard.

After political independence, this conditioning has continued. The visible symbol of this is the famous Kamuzu Academy at Mtunthama in Kasungu District. Kamuzu Academy was the President's (Dr Kamuzu Banda) dream and what he considered a legacy for the Youth of Malawi. It was patterned after some of the most elite public schools in Britain like Eton. Worse still, there was to be no Malawian teacher in the school. The President used to say that they were not educated enough, because they lacked classical education. What an insult to the people of Malawi! For all purposes, the school is a massive irrelevance in education theory and practice, a waste of money, and a monument to the glory of one person and not much of a heritage for the youth of Malawi. It is a white elephant that siphoned off much of the needed educational funds from other institutions.

If Malawi is to realise its intellectual independence, that is rooted primarily in its cultural soil, it will have to break out of this educational conditioning. Malawi will have to discover its own epistemological emphasis just as the Greeks, Romans, Germans, British and Americans have done. One that sustains its view of *uMunthu* rather than one that services capitalist needs at the expense of human well-being. It has to be an epistemological system that is distinctly Malawian. It is my conviction that while critical and scientific rationalism has proved very effective, it is not fit for Malawi, but rather wisdom for humanness (*Mahala gha Bunthu*, as it is said in Chindali and Chitumbuka or *Nzeru za uMunthu* in Chichewa). This is so because it is possible to be rational and yet be unwise, but it is impossible to be wise and irrational. The latter would be a contradiction in terms. While rationalism focuses on conceptual clarity and logical coherence, wisdom focuses on the choosing of right (just) means for right (just) ends at the right time and place for the common and communal good. Wisdom has to do with the propriety of character without negating rationalism. Rationalism is servant to wisdom and not the other way round.

When it came to spirituality or religion, critical rationalism raised fundamental problems which have resulted in the marginalization of this aspect of our experience and the stunted development of our *uMunthu*. It has caused human spirituality to be reduced to psychology and ethics leaving human beings compartmentalized and crying for a sense of wholeness, their *uMunthu*. Because there seems to be nothing to unify all these different and specialised compartments into a single whole we call *Munthu*, and there seems to be nothing to relate this *Munthu* to the rest of the cosmos, human beings look for fulfilment in drugs, alcohol, money and sex. The reaction of Romanticism to rationalism tells us of the inadequacy of this epistemological view point as the be all and end all. The human spirit refuses to be so confined. The enthronement of rationalism has left the Church in the West confused and without a solid place to stand in proclaiming its message. All other disciplines have made claims to some rational authorities and experts while the church's spiritual concerns have been rationally taken away by psychology and social work in areas where at one time it had been most effective.

The effect of critical and scientific rationalism on theology has been to drive it farther and farther away from the existential reality of God in Christ Jesus resulting in the spread of secularism, the death of God theologies, and the scientification of theology itself. However, the more this is done, the more the gospel message loses its vitality and becomes mechanistic. Malawi needs a theology that is based on wisdom of humanness (*mahala* or *nzeru*). This wisdom is related to the wisdom of God which in many ways is diametrically opposed to rationalism and transcends it. It was the prophet Isaiah who drew the sharpest contrast between human and God's wisdom.

> For my thoughts are not your thoughts, nor are your ways my ways, says the LORD. For as the heavens are higher than the earth, so are my ways higher than your ways and my thoughts than your thoughts (Isa 55:8f).

It is the apostle Paul who declared:

> For since, in the wisdom of God, the world did not know God through wisdom. God decided through the foolishness of our procla-

> mation to save those who believe .... For God's wisdom is wiser than human wisdom, and God's weakness is stronger than human strength (1 Cor 1:21,25).

By emphasizing on wisdom in the doing of theology, we touch on the wisdom of God and become open to the logic of God which transcends and redeems all systems of human logic of which formal and symbolic logic are only one form.

While rationalism has been successful at analysing, dissecting and debunking, it has failed miserably at working out a synthesis of human relationality in knowledge, let alone in being. Robert Bellah, an American social critique, and his colleagues have observed:

> There is widespread feeling that the promise of the modern era is slipping away from us. A movement of the enlightenment and liberation that was to have freed us from superstition and tyranny has led in the twentieth century to a world in which ideological fanaticism and political oppression have reached extremes unknown in previous history. Science which was to unlock the bounties of nature, has given us the power to destroy all life on earth. Progress, modernity's master idea, seems less compelling when it appears that it may be progress into the abyss.[20]

The problem with rationalism lies in its pretended autonomy and claim to universal sovereignty and adequacy as a way of knowing and consequently of living. This pretended autonomy goes against the wisdom of Malawians captured in the proverbs: *Nzeru za yekha anaviika nsima mmadzi* (a person who claims to be wise in one's own eyes will throw away golden opportunities); *Chala chimodzi sichiswa nsabwe* (One finger does not destroy a louse or certain tasks cannot be accomplished single-handedly); and *Mutu umodzi susenza denga* (One head does not lift a roof). The failure of rationalism to acknowledge other ways of knowing meant its own impoverishment. Charles Dickens, the British novelist, portrayed this poverty of rationalism in "The Hard Times". In philosophy we see the limitations of rationalism in the absurdity of the verification principle as it falls on its own face. Quoting Toumlin, Bellah points out:

---

20 Robert Bellah, et al., *Habits of the Heart: Individualism and Commitment in American Life*, New York: Harper & Row, 1985, p. 277.

> We can no longer view the world as Descartes and Laplace would have us do, as 'rational onlookers' from outside. Our place is within the same world that we are studying, and whatever scientific understanding we achieve must be a kind of understanding that is available to participants within the processes of nature, i.e. from inside.[21]

It is no wonder many in the West have to look to Eastern mysticism in an attempt to fulfil their spiritual quest. Within the controlling context of rationalism, western Christian spirituality could not meet that need. It had to be rationalized or else it could not meet the rationality test. To have it rationalized was to run the danger of turning it into either a philosophical or theological ideology or a mixture of the two which satisfied the minds in the way mathematics does, but left the heart dry.

Rationalism is only one way of knowing albeit a very useful and productive way. Its absolutization and, therefore, denial of other ways of spiritual and theological certitude has only helped to impoverish the human spirit. Without wholeness of knowledge, human beings can never be whole. To achieve wholeness of knowledge, all means of knowing have to be made available to and affirmed by human beings. This is possible if one is concerned with a view of life that is total and not partial. The problem with rationalism is that it is partial. The life experience of the Malawians is much wider than the concerns of rationalism to the point that rationalism cannot always be a competent judge over what we truly experience and know, and let alone to sit in judgment even over other cultural ways of knowing.

Rationalism puts a lot of premium on objectivity or propositional knowledge. It does not seem to see the symbolic nature of mathematical knowledge. Taking mathematics as the standard of certain knowledge, rationalism seeks to make all knowledge equally certain. There is nothing wrong with this, but the question is how. In search of such ground of objectivity, Descartes bifurcated nature, the head was severed from the heart, and he did not know how to put it together again. All that he succeeded in proving was the fact that objectivity in knowledge is possible only from a subjective base. This is the only thing that can be said about both his dictum *Cogito ergo sum* and the process by which he arrives at it.

---

21 *Ibid.*, p. 283.

The other problem of rationalism is to view the subjective and the objective as opposites thus creating an unnecessary dualism. Why can't they be viewed as two sides of the same coin, which are complementary, but not identical, and to be explained one in terms of the other? Objective concepts are only abstractions of subjective knowledge. Rationalism left to reign as sovereign over the realm of knowledge leaves it a landscape of dualisms in eternal conflict. As the saying goes, "when two elephants fight, it is the grass that suffers". Similarly, when a duality is in conflict, it is the humans that suffer by becoming schizoid. It is impossible to find wholeness and, therefore, also life's authentic meaning in such a universe. Since rationalism apes its mathematical image after which it is patterned, it tends toward abstractions divorced from existential experience in spite of the fact that it is this experience that fuels its insatiable intellectual appetite. Since rationalism, in its pretended autonomy, is sovereign, only those who are initiated in its ways can be recognized as cultured, civilised, and truly enlightened while the rest are relegated to the position of fiends, heathens and pagans.

It is to the benefit of humanity, especially marginalised humanity, that rationalism has of late been seen for what it really is, and that is, a partial view of knowing being paraded as the only way and thus privileging those who have developed and benefitted from it with an unfair advantage and a false sense of their own *uMunthu*. The questioning of Eurocentrism is not only a political, economic, and curricular concern, but one of epistemology. It is only those who are going to open up to other possibilities that stand to experience a true liberation from the confines of ethnocentrism. We are the richer from learning from other people as long as they do not consider it foolishness, but wisdom for so doing. It is not surprising then that it is those who have learned from rationalism who find it inadequate and who want to make their own perspectives available to the rest of the world by being inclusive. Afro-centrism is one case in point.

The problem that I see with Afro-centrism is that it runs the danger of articulating itself in terms of European rationalism and not African wisdom and insight in its multi-symbolic character. Jean-Marc Ela, the Cameroonian Roman Catholic theologian has well observed:

> the African civilization is a civilization of symbols .... As a result to deprive Africans of their essential symbols also deprives them of their self-awareness and tears them from the reality that has inte-

> grated them into the very system by which, through its symbols, they are striving to overcome the contradiction between life and death.[22]

It may be hard for Afro-centrism to avoid this trap since writing was effectively introduced to most of Africa by Europeans. However, it is folly for non-Africans to deny Afro-centricity a place as not providing an enrichment to human wholeness.

For Malawi, we will need more ways of knowing than strictly rationalism. We will seek to transcend rationalism as we best know how. Since the major concern of Malawians is *uMunthu*, the epistemological emphasis falls on wisdom. For Malawians, wisdom has to do with choosing right means and right ends for the good of the community. This means that there is much more involved than simply intellectual knowledge. It has to do with the pragmatism of *uMunthu*. It includes intellectual knowledge (both theoretical and practical), relational knowledge (physical and spiritual), embodied knowledge (integrity and productivity), intuitive knowledge (feelings, faith, hope, dreams), mythical knowledge, and narrative knowledge (proverbs, stories, songs), in short, the whole of life. All these are there to service life or *uMunthu* and not simply to be focussed on as functional ends in themselves, an attitude which has been responsible for much fragmentation and rugged individualism in the West. We need to take responsibility for what we know, that is, to embody it and be accountable for it, rather than remain indifferent to it. That responsibility is possible only by tying knowledge to *uMunthu*.

The passing of traditions from generation to generation has been through oral narrative. Narrative has always included factual information, myth, story, poetry, song, proverbs, drama and dance. Narrative has insisted on the maximum dramatization of life as captured through word. The fundamental goal of this transmission of tradition has always been wisdom. The skills to be acquired were the ability to discern wisdom in the stories so as to distill and appropriate it. The emulation of the good in the story or song, and the avoidance of the bad accounted for wisdom. Proverbs proved to be the ready vehicles for distilled wisdom, and the task of education was to learn their appropriate application. Myths had to do with cosmological

---

22 Jean-Marc Ela, *My Faith as an African*, Maryknoll: Orbis; London: Geoffrey Chapman, 1988, p. 35.

and historical wisdom, while proverbs related more to existential principles.

If wisdom is the controlling element rather than rationality, knowledge is not an end in itself, but is acquired to serve a way of life - a wise way of living - *uMunthu* and for the establishment of *Muzi Uweme* (the Good Community). Wisdom unrelated to *uMunthu* and the Good Community is inconceivable. Foolishness is either a sign of immaturity or serious mental deformity. To insist on wisdom is not to reject rationalism, but to deny its controlling status. Wisdom is the totality of one's being, seeking to be properly in tune with its total environment, visible and invisible.

Rational propositions are not adequate ways of transmitting living wisdom. Their form, patterned on mathematical and physical sciences, is meant to deal only with either abstract or frozen reality, but not life as lived. It is not surprising then, that anything having to do with life as it is, is relegated to practical theology or ethics. The fact that God is living and active is made abstract and treated as a metaphor or concept and not the very ground of people's daily lives. A theology concerned with proofs of God's existence betrays this mathematical and scientific bias. The inscrutability of God as testified to in scripture can only come from a God one relates to personally, than from one rationally established. To rely entirely on rational presentation of God is to limit the reality of God.

Life as lived moves on a number of levels of experience, knowledge, and logic, of which rationality and its logic of meaningful language and coherence is only one. Narrative is the most suited means of conveying wisdom because it provides live scenes with which the listener interacts as they enlighten his/her own life and world. More often than not, the listener is always on the lookout for highlights of *uMunthu*. He/she will try to discriminate between those characters that portray the negative aspects of *uMunthu* and identify himself or herself with the positive or appropriate characters of *uMunthu* that are portrayed in the stories as a dictate of wisdom. Stories dramatize life and human characters, while the onlookers or listeners can identify with the stories at different levels of perception.

Wisdom is communal and has to do with the survival and well being of the individual and community. It is the community that eventually decides what is wisdom and what is not. Rational discourse is too rigid, complicated and elitist in its logic as to benefit only a few and is limited when it comes to dealing with the flow of life. One can be rational, but not committed to a rational way of life. To be committed to wisdom is to be committed to a lifestyle of *uMunthu* in the world. To abandon wisdom is to opt for foolishness and, therefore, an empty humanity. The Tumbuka have a phrase for this, it is called *Chinthu cha waka*, meaning, "a useless thing".

Since theology has fallen victim to the exclusive claims of critical rationalist thought, even though the biblical source of theology is all narrative, theology becomes the preserve only of the initiated, an elitist club that specializes in matters that have been abstracted out of life. However, the reality is that it is not only the initiated who ask theological questions and need theological answers, it is all the living who are asking about the meaning of their lives or *uMunthu*. Therefore, theology in Malawi will have to be such that it responds to the questions of the ordinary people concerning their personal and communal relationship with God and with each other as they live their lives each day. The wise thing to do is to talk about their *uMunthu* because God, other human beings and the environment converge around that reality.

There is a corollary to this. Apart from scripture, the other major source of theology in Malawi has to be the lives of the people themselves as historically lived and reflected in their oral and written literature. Contrary to Paul Tillich, the correlation is not between questions of culture and answers of theology, but rather, human life and God's life. The question is a tool of life and the answer is there to service life. Life understood as *uMunthu* is the cornerstone for our theological task in Malawi.

In cooking African theology, several factors need to be taken into account. The first is that of our Africanness. It is generally assumed that we know and understand what this means, but the truth is that most of us do not. The fact that we have been brought up living the African way does not mean that we understand its reality. There is need to reflect on our African way of life so as to discover those fundamental principles upon which it is based. However, one needs to be cautious in the way that reflection takes place. Since most of us have been trained in western ways of reflection, we tend to impose on the African way western canons of thought and end up seeing African reality as if it were western reality. African reflection calls for new epistemological approaches that would lead to discovering African reality. What are some of these epistemological consideration? The west has founded its philosophical outlook on rationalism, that is, the need to observe the law of non-contradiction, logical coherence, and objectivity. While these have their place, as Africans, these are found to be wanting because they do not cover the whole of our experience. I have come up with what I call ontological cognition as the way into knowledge. Ontological cognition is based on ontological relationality as a way of being in the world. Ontological cognition privileges wisdom over rationalism. One can be rational and yet unwise, but one cannot be wise and irrational at the same time. Rationality is considered an aspect of wisdom because its wisdom has got to do with life as a whole and not simply with thought. While rationalism has tended to lead to dichotomies, ontological cognition reconciles these dichotomies and sees them as two sides of the same coin.

Theology Cooked in an African Pot

B.S. Chuba

One day a couple from New Zealand visited us in a temporary Scottish home at our invitation for a special meal. At capturing a smell of the food which was anxiously awaiting them, they each remarked: "hhh, delicious!" to which remark my wife replied, "We had thought of making you a delicious Zambian meal, but this is all we could do after improvising the ingredients. It could have been better, you know! Had it been cooked using a full Zambian recipe." The couple quickly retorted, "Please give us your recipe, we would like to try it too".

"Theology cooked (or boiling) in an African pot!" This is a fascinating theme for us, particularly to an old African who has tasted food cooked in an African way, for cooking the African way takes time and patience. Those African (mothers) who cook it use familiar ingredients, and the cooking is done by those nurtured in local techniques accumulated over many enlightened years.

The theme, "Theology cooked in an African pot", is itself strictly a new [perhaps amplified] definition of African Christian theology. It can therefore find its place in the definition of the total enterprise of theology. John Macquarrie, defines theology as:

> The study [about God] which, through participation in and reflection upon a religious faith seeks to express the content of this faith in the clearest and most coherent language available.[1]

Though Charles Nyamiti,[2] J.C. Thomas (Anglican clergy),[3] and other African theologians give similar definitions of African theology, we would safely begin our discussion from John Macquarrie's, because we do not want to create an impression that African Christian theology is designed to be so peculiar to an African that it cannot be conducive to the universal

---

1 John Macquarrie, *Principles of Christian Theology*, New York: Charles Scribner's, 1996, p. 1.

2 Charles Nyamiti, *The Way to Christian Theology for Africa*, Eldoret: Gaba Publ., nd. p. 1.

3 J.C. Thomas, *Ghana Bulletin of Theology*, Vol. 1, No. 4, pp. 14, 16, 20-21.

theological academy and ecclesia. It is not meant to be a theology in which other ethnic or racial groups cannot feel at home. Rather, what should mark it uniquely and genuinely peculiar is that, as much as possible:

(a) Its context is African
(b) Its language is African
(c) Its advocates are Africans themselves
(d) Its target (resultant object of faith) is African

A theology cooked in an African pot is therefore, in my opinion, a theology relevant and conducive to a particular context, fully nurtured and keenly participated in by the indigenous without excluding the participation of peoples from other contexts.

1. Theology in a Context

Issues about African Theology have been discussed, sometimes with over enthusiasm, by many patriotic African theologians. African Theology continues to be discussed from academic podiums, from pulpits and through books which still flood the world bookstalls. But, the worrying issue today is how seriously the propounded issues have been believed by advocates of this theology, and when the many useful ideas advanced from discussions will be put to productive use in the so called main line churches led by the advocates themselves, in the same way they are powerfully put to practical use in the emerging Independent Churches led by those who do not go out preaching about it.

If a theology (the study about God) calls for participation in and reflection upon a religious faith, then advocates of African theology (theology cooked in an African pot) ought to take it as a practical exercise rather than as a theoretical or purely academic exercise, and it should be seen to be influencing the daily lives of their growing communities. And if through that participation in and reflection upon the Christian faith we seek to express the content of the faith in a language which makes sense to the community in which it is expressed, then we must use the tools common and intelligible to both the listeners and the conveyors of the content of that faith. Hence the concept of contextualisation. Contextualisation is putting an element, a thing or practice to suit the context it is meant to serve, thus making it relevant and conducive to participation in that particular context. At the same time contextualisation, wider in scope then indigenization, opens up and allows for the inclusion, into (African) Christian practice, of other relevant elements from the rich communities of the modern world. This happens as a particular context in its development comes into a testing contact with other communities. It consequently subjects its practices to logical readjustment so as to make Christianity relevant to that growing context. During that process there is meant to be an inevitable re-examination, pruning and purification of the African content with the saving Gospel, without necessarily obliterating it.

For a long time, Africans shamelessly believed that they have little to offer to the world outside their own, that what they have is inferior or that it is not good enough. This has often proved to be a timid belief and at its worst hypocritical. For when the same Africans are pressed further into realistic action in worship or in daily life they produce the expressions which are clearly their own. One of the tools that would help us to see an African in his/her proper personality is music. Although an African sings meticulously from hymn books made of dry, translated orthodox foreign hymns, he quickly throws down to the seat the book when an African tune is called. Then both the hands, the feet and the mouth begin to sing the tune in concert. It quickly becomes known that through music Africans express their deep feelings more than they can utter them normally and through it instruct and correct those doing wrong. Most African royal singers praise and reprimand even their Paramount Chiefs through songs.

It is the down-to-earth theology in the hymns of African Independent Churches that is appealing more to a cross section of African communities today. J.H. Nketia once wrote: "What good is it to the African to come regularly to a service conducted in a language and musical idiom which he does not understand?"[4]

When an African pretends to use tools to express his faith the owners of the foreign tools simply laugh. Mabel Shaw, an educational LMS missionary once observed this among the boys and girls at her mission station at Mbereshi:

> The boys and girls were singing lustily and not untunefully a translation of an English hymn "Welcome happy morning", the song of greeting to the returning chief. They stood in untidy rows. The only woman in the front stood: the rest, thinking themselves unseen, remained seated. They did not know the words; the tune was strange, they were entirely uninterested .... There seemed little

> reality in it. Those very women had been full of life and joy only a few days previously, when they had welcomed a returning missionary with song and dance, with rhythmic clapping of hands and stamping of feet. I had seen them greet Chief Kazembe again and again by lifting the right hand and with the left tapping the mouth to make that curiously pleasing greeting (*akapundu*), which is the women's peculiar greeting.[5]

Indeed the African expressions for greetings are peculiarly African and are symbolically graded. For instance, you do not normally greet with the left hand but the right, or you greet with both hands, or you greet shaking hands twice, and sometimes you genuflect, or you prostrate etc. All these are symbolisms conveying great contextual meanings. If this is what makes sense to an African, let it be offered freely to God. And they are already doing it in Independent Churches. One Zionist Church service in Palapye (Botswana) begins with the congregation singing a moving song facing the cross as they genuflect with the clapping of hands, to greet the Lord the African way.

Bishop Peter Sarpong of Ghana once made similar sentiments to the fact that it is easier and necessary to express oneself to God in one's own language.

> The Christian at worship must give of his best - our best is our own culture that makes meaning to us without limitations.[6]

The relevance of contextualization in theology as in other spheres of African life is that contextualization will trigger a productive change in an African's attitude to Christianity. It will clarify the Christian practices which have for so long been required to conform to the missionary format, which has consequently been associated with the West (which I refer to as the North).

This has also been the concern expressed by the right thinking missionaries of the century. We are all worried about the obscurity of African worship (for instance its, holy communion elements), and about African politics, education, church administration etc., which have followed the patterns alien and often unintelligible to an African. Africans have not been

---

4 J.H. Nketia, *International Review of Missions*, vol. 47, 1958, pp. 265ff.

5 Mabel Shaw, *God's Candlelights*, London: Edinburgh House Press, 1939, pp. 18f.

6 Peter Sarpong, *African Theological Journal*, Accra: June 1972.

honest enough to their own forms of expression. Their minds have been enslaved in the mystery of what, historically, they have inherited, and they have believed, blindly, to nullify even whatever little they have conserved in their culture. Donald Fraser, a Church of Scotland missionary, was at one point equally concerned about this with regard to music:

> Why should African musical have its songs of praise given in a music which is entirely foreign? While all village life is full of tuneful African music, why should not the gospel not only use idiomatic vernacular for its proclamation but also idiomatic African music.[7]

We must persistently make full use of indigenous tools in paying our homage to God and in explaining our faith in him to the world because it is biblically justified. Scripture allows that Jews and Gentiles practice their Christian faith from their own Christian camps with their own Christian camping equipments and within their camp climates and vegetations (Gal. 2:14b, Gal. 3:27ff). But also, of course, the idea is truly missionary oriented. Missionaries that traversed the world were sent out in order to go and help establish Christ's Church among peoples of different cultural backgrounds and leave them to deal with Christ himself, concerning any details of their types of participation in worship, administrations and language of expression and so on. For instance, in the 1894 "rules of Livingstonia missionaries", concerning the organization of the local churches in their mission fields, it was stated thus:

> It is desirable that as far as possible the native church should have freedom to develop according to its natural surroundings and circumstances rather than that it should be constrained into rigid conformity with the home churches without their past historical development: (1) that the mission council form the connecting link with the home churches [in UK], (2) that in the organization and development of the native church self-support shall be the standard of self government.[8]

---

7 Donald Fraser, "The Evangelistic Approach to the African", *International Review of Missions*, Vol. 15, 1926, p. 447.

8 Free Church of Scotland, *Church of Scotland Rules for the Guidance of Missionaries from Scotland. Rules for Livingstonia Missionaries; Organization of the Native Church*, Edinburgh: National Library of Scotland, 1894.

The LMS had also made it clear that they were going out on mission not to further denominationalism but to establish an indigenous church for the indigenous and eventually by the indigenous people. They were to go and plant, and not necessarily to stay and water, on the pattern of St Paul's theology of mission.

> I planted, Apollos watered, but God gave the growth. So neither he who plants nor he who waters is anything, but only God who gives the growth.[9]

Indeed, the principal purpose of the Christian mission beginning with Christ himself was to help build the church that would eventually grow, by God's own grace, to be self supporting, self controlling and self propagating. The youthful missionaries who were scattered out of the North on mission to many lands were cautioned against departing from this norm. But, as Martin Luther puts it, "Human nature is like a drunk peasant. Lift him into the saddle on one side, over he topples on the other side."[10] It is human nature to think wisely and act selfishly. Consequently, some of them went out to serve and stay put; settle, and naturally they were instinctively tempted to begin setting up carbon copies of their home chapels, liturgies, bureaucracies and theological conceptions, as much of them as they could remember, which linger on in the mission fields to this day. The result is that most of the African Church has no theology but that of the London Camp or the Paris camp or the Vatican See or the Lambeth Conference. This is an extent that, instead of the drum calling us to worship, we must, at all cost and in search of prestige, import a bell from bell casters in London and when old ones get broken, foreign currency must be found to import replacements. Our Bishops' rings must come from overseas, so are the Holy Communion vessels and the liturgies with them. The Holy God lives up there and only visits us here to see how we are faring, so we think, because we cannot live with him permanently here! And so we must learn the language of our friends there (and we have done so more expertly than we have managed our own). Our theological syllabuses should come from there. An African has believed and defied

---

9 1 Corinthians 3:6.

10 Tony Castle, *The Hodder Book of Christian Quotations*, London: Hodder and Stoughton, 1982, p. 120.

Rome and Canterbury and Geneva as the only Christian Citadels! Robert Shepherd was right when he wrote:

> The Banthu, like Athenians, love any "new thing", and are perhaps the most imitative race on earth. Sometimes these characteristics show themselves in harmless form, as in the names they choose to give their children. Almost every child baptized into the Christian Church is given an English name, sometimes of the strangest kind. "Orienda", "Elberthial", "Dorathina", "Glory", "M. Glory", "Time-keeper".[11]

The concept propagated here is and seems to have been, and may continue to be, that an African's name cannot be Christian but an English or other foreign name. Yet in a theology cooked in an African pot, no African name should be foreign to God. God knows, Peter just as much as he knows Zulu or Mabengano or Mudede or Botha or Masire or Ndhlovu.

Archbishop Desmond Tutu was once quoted by a Church of Scotland preacher from a pulpit as having said:

> When missionaries came they had a Bible and we had the land. When they said, "Let us pray" we closed our eyes. When we opened them they had all the land and we had the Bible in our hands.

The land was lost and it took long to get it back. I pray that we will pray with our eyes open or at least not close them too tightly.

When the creatures in the universe praise and pray to God, God listens to them all. He knows all the language and though forms. To him no language or any kind of voice in the world is without significance. And when he speaks they listen and understand him in their various ethnic groupings. One broadcaster once said that the way we perceive things depends on where we are; that is our cultural environment which affects our perception. Hence we human beings make our worlds primarily from what we know; from our contexts. This also means that all that we use, all that is around and about our living is language. Language can be vocal, instrumental or simply acted. All these create the world we live in. Hence it is complex, if not impossible, to measure one's reasoning from any other ground than one's own. There is no culture from which you can judge the other. We make mistakes daily when we measure the excellence of other

---

11 Robert H.W. Shepherd, *The Banthu*, Edinburgh: UFCS Publications Department, 1927, p. 85.

people's cultural standards from our stand point, as if ours is the best. In the same way we make a mistake if we think our cultural standard is inferior to the other because the other looks and sounds more prominent. Each cultural language should feel confident and ripe enough to set up its own standard of excellency. Then it will benefit the wider world.

In any case the universal God begins where we are. Because we appreciate him in our own situations, we realize he can be sufficient for us and so we begin to learn, out of his love, to avail his sufficiency to others through our mission.

Perhaps, what precipitates on an already irritated sore is that this perpetuation of foreign tools at the expense of our African context, is still upheld by us African Christian leaders as well as our Christians, sometimes even more zealously than missionaries themselves. This is what can be referred to as blind Christian zeal than has no roots, and therefore renders itself impotent to promote local growth.

2. Theology in the Clearest and most Coherent Language

It is becoming evident today that numerically African Independent Churches are the fastest growing Christian Communities on this continent, despite their inadequate literacy and leadership force. One of the reasons for this is that these Churches are speaking a language to the adherents which can be easily understood. Not only are they able to use the God-given tools [hands, rattles, drums etc.] available to them with much more effect, but their songs [hymns] are themselves preached sermons. These are sung to put across to their members, in a vivid and forceful way, theological conceptions of themes such as God, salvation, sin, repentance, love, politics etc., which are at the very heart of African concerns. They translate the cultural potency of these themes into the Christian church, giving them a new intelligible and contextual meaning. They, thus, use local languages to articulate their faith.

The culture of a particular people, whether in politics or in Christianity, gives that people the meaningful identity. Among the elements that form the culture of a people are; disciplinary codes, moral conduct in society, the means employed for human survival, tools of a people in their everyday living. Included in these are elements valued by a community such as courteous behaviour towards all, especially the elderly and the women, chivalry and family fecundity, patriotism and African self-reliance, and a whole range of scientific knowledge. We would take into account also the artistic language expressions, the knowledge of botany, handicraft and technical skills, and drama. These and many other elements prop up a culture which is continually reshaped in the course of the development of a community. These, which are often referred to as elements of a people's heritage, are handed down from generation to generation and are tried and retried until proved viable and conducive to that particular community. All Africans have, directly or indirectly, passed through this handing and taking over process. It is in such a community with such a rich (retried) culture that Christianity must prove itself complementary rather than antagonistic, sanctifying and not destructive. In this way an African will live a dignified, distinctive and contributing life in the world of many cultures. An African should therefore be urged, and if found slumbering, be pushed, to wake up to this challenge to put across to the world, beginning from where he/she is, the gospel into that rich (retried) language which is coherent to the African listener.

An example of one Independent Church would suffice to indicate considerable success in contextualization and to show how in indigenous language has proved to be more attractive to a cross section of Africans. This was the Lumpa Church in Zambia, led by an illiterate woman, Lenshina Mulenga Lubusha. In terms of the interpretations of theological concepts (on God, sin, salvation, stewardship, Christian practices), she overwhelmed the main-line churches. Theirs was theology cooked or boiling in the African pot. The Lubwa Church of the Church of Scotland, for instance, became empty because all or most of its Christians joined her church.

But perhaps the major problem in Africa's quest for contextualization has been that an average African Christian has been embarrassingly overwhelmed by the outside world. He/she has the tendency to gullibly grab any fashionable thing/style that is enchanting in his/her eyes and is easily persuaded to believe, often with no good reason, that his own resources are not as good, as mature and as Christian as those that come from elsewhere, as we have seen in the case of names. It is disappointing that when the churches of the North change, for instance, from old patterns of Christian worship, the African Churches are busy taking on the old skins thrown away by their friends in the North. Africa has become a dumping ground for theologies because she does not believe she has any of her own.

Africa has abandoned her own and so lost many invaluable cultural elements. Indeed if the African himself/herself does not value and respect his/her cultural elements, who else will respect and value them? An African who neglects his/her own values will only know his/her folly in the dying moments of his/her life, as John Mbiti states in a Ugandan saying: "The cow knows not what her tail is worth till she has lost it."

3. Africans will themselves have to be advocates of theology cooked in an African pot

We know that the political, economic and social situations of independent Africa have been disappointingly retrogressive and have adversely affected other institutions including the Church. There have been many reasons for this, including dishonest management, irresponsible borrowing and at its worst, shameless borrowing from rich nations. Independent Africa has sold its dignity and consequently lost its destiny.

This has adversely affected the African Church too. Christians in Africa are engaged in an endless quest for a meaningful "African theology of self-reliance". Indeed, with all the abundant natural resources in space, soil, sea and human body, God does not expect Africa to be trotting round the globe from Frankfurt to Moscow, from Paris to Geneva, from London to New York, from Tokyo to Beijing (Peking) with a poor man's enamel plate begging! Any nation which turns itself into a begging nation cannot command respect. Beggars are never respected anywhere. They cannot speak out at important forums. They are expected to keep quiet and to wait to be given. The rich nations are ruling the world. So one superpower can shut down the heavens and stop them from bringing down rains on the fourteen or more poor folk, and cause them to tremble and suffocate. That African dependency is the most humiliating kind of slavery. Yet we know that "no man loves his slave fetters, be they be made of Gold". No receiver should take pride in being a perpetual mendicant beggar! We know that addicted givers would wish to give until they find themselves totally dehumanizing the receiver. The African Church needs to rediscover an African theology of self-reliance. Each African nation, let alone African Church, has to seriously and strenuously strive for means to attain self-reliance, in the pattern of the African heritage. Under the indigenous African heritage, in an

African village, every able bodied person (man, woman) was expected to be self-supporting and patriotic, able to share with others whatever fruits they had of their or their families' labours. Only when Africa shall learn to produce and profitably exchange with the world shall she command substantial respect and claim to be a good steward of God's abundant gifts. The 21st century must see Africa developing a theology of self reliance, for "he who depends on another dines ill and sups worse". *Alya amakombesha*, 'he ends up eating left overs'. Moreover, would there be any justification today for why the already independent Africa (since the 1950s) and her Church, should perpetuate the "feed me", "support me", "do it for me" mentality which should be long gone by now? Why should Africa continue to condone the impotence portrayed by its leaders at OAU and other organizations, when Africans are known for their sense of a united, sharing and corporate community? With clean, great and mighty rivers: the Nile, the Niger, the Limpopo, the Luapula-Lualaba-Congo, the Zambezi etc., Africans, in their own right minds, should not die of thirst and hunger while their waters laughingly flow their wealth away into seas and oceans on both sides. Does Africa not boast of the great lakes: Victoria, Chad, Malawi, Volta, Tanganyika, Turkana and many more, most of them full of fresh waters and fleshy fishes? Does Africa not have vast lands with immense treasure in, under and above them, known and not yet known? And does Africa not contain, in addition, the rare metals (uranium), precious metals (gold, platinum, silver), chemical and fertilizer mineral (phosphate), base metals (lead, zinc, copper, tin), ferro-alloy metals (chromium, cobalt, manganese, vanadium, nickel), iron, light metal (aluminum), diamonds and most hopefully many more that have not yet been exploited?

O free and rich Africa, yet sleepy Africa.
How are the mighty fallen (in their Africa)
and the weapons of war perished (Sam 1:27).
Debts upon debts and grants on top of grants
that yield no self-reliance,
it is still all poverty, politically and ecclesiastically.
O God, we pray, redeem Africa your own way.
Yes, I belong to you, my Africa,
yet I hate to belong to lazy minded you.
They envy you, Africa, but you do not realize your worth in you.

The invaluable resources in and beside you;
Come on Africans!
Stand up like real men - you Africans!
Act for Africa they should respect for ever
let there be in you a vision for ever
or else you remain for ever a wretched laughing stock.
For people perish into nothingness
who have no vision within themselves
or a common good for themselves.
Yet I say to you, my Africa, if your redeemer lives,
show the world now, not tomorrow,
that he really lives, in you and your marrow.[12]

Having said this, I must also emphasize that the time to cry over spilt milk is over. Now is the time to implement the theological vision towards growth. We have done enough talking at conferences like this one. We must begin to implement in the clearest language, in the simplest language and in the most useful language for ordinary Africans to follow our thinking. We have to shift from mere academic exercises to real applied theology. The onus to develop a relevant African Christian theology finally and practically rests with the Africans let alone African theologians themselves. We must begin from this notion because this is what will inevitably lead us into a deeper quest for contextualization. Moreover, as we have observed earlier, societies on earth are like camps. They belong to one and same master/commander. But they are placed in different environments where they are encountering life in different ways. As they serve their one master using different methods, they are bound to produce different results, but all to please the same master. Inevitably, each society, in its own camp, has its special values [the heritage of the people] which may often look and sound unintelligible to other societies. The sane values may be respected and admired elsewhere. Hence in Africa, for example, what may be innocently viewed as good and courteous manners may be misconstrued elsewhere as very bad or rude manners. For example, I was travelling on a plane to Manila (Philippines). On the plane was a pamphlet on "Hints on Filipino culture", for guidance of foreigners visiting the Philippines; I got interested

[12] The author has devised this heart-felt poem to bring to bear the frustration that has erupted in the hearts of many as a result of negligence of the Africans, especially the intelligentsia, who like to just talk and talk.

in some of them listed here;

1. Respect for age is an important priority.
2. Giving food to the sick is more appropriate than giving flowers. The latter is associated with death.
3. Don't use your finger in an upward position to call someone to you. It is very degrading. Beckon with the hand in a downward motion.

These few hints struck some meaning to me from another traditional society. I do not know if they would have much meaning to an indigenous English friend beyond being just meaningful and helpful hints for survival only among the Filipino.

4. The target (object) of African theology (theology cooked in an African pot) is an African

This theology is not to be abstract. Rather it should aim to serve God's purpose among his people, especially the underprivileged Africans. In practical terms it must enter boldly into areas where other theologies would not venture. It must seek to address issues at stake in the lives of the African people such as:

a) Need for unity, especially in times of social, political, economic crises, including the discussion of God's tools on earth that should catalyze this, such as OAU, AACC, ecumenical bodies etc., which point to unity.
b) Concern for the breakdown of the powerful African sense of community life and its extended family and communal living based on the African concept of sacrifice, (that none lives to himself/herself) - which is itself a Christian principle.
c) The basic rights of people in debtor countries to food, shelter, clothing, employment, primary health care and conducive environment.
d) The concept of interdependency rather than dependence, emanating from the notions of self-reliance (economical), self propagating (evangelical), and self governing (administrative).

Africans need a theology that will redeem them from the "give me", "teach me" and "lead me" mentality, especially at this age of an independent Africa (in church and politics). Where a theology does not serve God's creation this way, that theology is more than dead. That theology which is not cooked or at least not boiling in an African pot has its abode in an African pit.

Theology Already Cooked in an African Pot

James N. Amanze

Akin Omoyajowo in his paper titled "An Expression of African Christianity" has reminded us that it is customary these days to hear people, both lay and cleric, describing Christianity as an "imported religion", the religion of the colonial masters and that quite often there is a general call to indigenize Christianity. Omoyajowo has argued that for many centuries the Christian Church in Africa has failed to Africanize itself fast and deep enough to ensure not only its continuity, but also to enhance its outlook as truly indigenous in Africa as it is truly indigenous in Europe and America. In his assessment the Christian Church in Africa, which produced distinguished theologians such as Tertullian, St Cyprian, St Augustine of Hippo and indeed many others, failed to Africanize the Christian Church in its theology and belief. In regard to these theologians, their beliefs, rituals and theological stance were essentially European. Their theologies addressed primarily the needs of the Roman and Greek middle classes that constituted the then African Church. Across the ages the church in Africa made very little attempt, if any, to cast off its foreign mantle and assume the African garment in order to present itself as an indigenous religion to the Africans.

Omoyajowo has observed that the foreignness of the church was more visible during the colonial era since the missionaries were, quite often, associated with the colonial masters. During much of this period, Christian Churches presented Christianity to the Africans not from an African perspective but from a European and American perspective. Their theologies were carbon copies of the theologies of their mother churches in England, Italy, Germany, United States of America and other countries overseas. In the second half of the 19th century, however, a new phenomenon emerged on the African continent, more particularly in Africa south of the Sahara. As the gospel spread far and wide in the remotest parts of Africa, many Africans began to recognize the relevance of Christianity in their own lives and consequently generated a desire to use the most effective methods to disseminate the gospel to fellow Africans. This they did by employing African culture to convey the fundamental truths of the Christian religion to their fellow Africans in a way that they could best understand and internalize the gospel truth as if it were one of the African indigenous religions. The beginning of Christianity in Africa was accompanied with prefabricated theologies and rituals which advocated the total eradication of African cultural values including the religious beliefs and practices of the African people, thus alienating them from the benefits of this world religion.[1] Omoyajowo puts it aptly thus:

> The God that was introduced to Africa was a completely foreign God and this robbed Christianity of its universality. Inspite of its civilizing and educating nature, this religion became spiritually unsatisfactory. The African could not really see its relevance to his life. The result was an ambivalent spiritual life. In times of crisis, the believer could revert back to traditional measures.[2]

There is a general agreement among African theologians that African Independent Churches have taken a daring step of contextualizing or indigenizing the Church in Africa. These churches, in their bid to make the Church relevant to the Africans in all aspects of their lives, are making use of their cultural religious heritage to explain a whole range of the doctrines of the Church in order to make the Good News of salvation accomplished by Jesus Christ easily understood by their fellow Africans. Consequently, they have produced a relevant theology for Africa. They have also succeeded in producing a ritual-oriented church which appeals to the deep-seated emotions of the African peoples and thus satisfying their spirituality. Kofi Appiah-Kubi has observed that among the Akan people of Ghana African Independent Churches have made "a conscious attempt to revive or perpetuate selected aspects of the Akan culture which is considered more satisfying than western patterns. By this noble and bold attempt these churches are meeting a need grossly ignored by the intellectualized Christianity of the missionary kind." [3] Harold Turner has it that the indigenization of the Church in Africa does not necessarily represent an attempt to escape from the scandal of the particular part that western and eastern people have played in the tremendous fact that Black Africa in less than two centuries has become the second major geographical - cultural area in the

---

1 A.J. Omoyajowo, "An African Expression of Christianity", in M. Motlhabi (ed), *Black Theology*, n.d., p. 62.

2 Ibid.

3 Kofi Appiah-Kubi, "Indigenous Christian Churches: Signs of Authenticity", in Kofi Appiah-Kubi & S. Torres (eds), *African Theology en Route*, Maryknoll: Orbis, 1979, p. 118.

whole history of Christian expansion, rather it is a need to entrench Christianity into the bowels of mother Africa so that it may remain here for ever.[4] Despite the dangers involved in indigenization, the African Independent Churches have remained basically Christian. G.C. Oosthuizen has observed that these churches "remain true to the basic creeds of the Christian faith and in the final analysis one will discover that many of the Independent Church movements are churches, where the Word is really preached and sacraments rightly administered".[5] M. L. Daneel's testimony of the sound theological nature of the African Independent Churches needs reference here. He writes:

> Despite the seemingly "heretical" notions held by many Independent Churches, they have - through their lives, both their earthly celebrations and their unquestionable awareness of God - made profoundly aware of what I consider to be the caring attitude of Christ.[6]

Drawing examples from Botswana it will be noted below that the Africanisation of the Church in the African Independent Churches in Botswana, both in terms of theology and rituals, is currently in full swing. Tswana, through local initiative and inspiration, have conjured up a brand of Christianity that is both African and Christian in nature. In this way they have produced an African form of Christianity which is widely accepted by many Tswana. Their appeal has been directed to the emotional needs of Tswana in the areas of faith healing, use of traditional medicine, divination, prophecy, veneration of the ancestors, spirit possession, dancing and clapping of hands during church services, observance of some rites of passage and agricultural rites while at the same time remaining essentially Christian in doctrine and faith without any dangers of syncretism.

Many African Independent Churches have retained most of the doctrines of the Christian Church but in communicating them to their people, they have borrowed very heavily from their own cultures to explain these doctrines to their fellow Africans in the simplest way possible. Doctrines such as the Trinity, christology, pneumatology, soteriology, missiology, ecclesiology, demonology, and many others are found in the African Independent Churches in varying degrees.

---

4 Harold Turner, "Reflections on African Movements During a Missiological Conference", in *Missionalia*, vol. 12, no. 3, 1984, p. 109.

5 G.C. Oosthuizen, *Post-Christianity in Africa*, Grand Rapids: Eerdmans, 1968, p. xiv.

6 M.L. Daneel, *Quest for Belonging*, Gweru: Mambo, 1987, p. 23.

1. Christology

(a) Mediator or intermediary

As a corollary of what has been said above, one of the most appealing and most powerful titles of Jesus in the African Independent Churches in Botswana is that of mediator or intermediary. Here the christology of the African Independent Churches assumes a full African mantle. The Biblical image of Christ as Mediator and Intercessor (Heb 7:25; 1 Tim 2:5) finds its strongest support in the African concept of ancestors among Tswana. The ancestors (*badimo*) have always assumed the role of mediators, intermediaries, intercessors and go-between God in heaven and people here below. No one can approach *Modimo* except through the *badimo*. Thus basing their understanding on the nature and work of Christ as described in some parts of the New Testament, the new churches quite often, conceive Jesus as the mediator between the Church and God. When people ask something from God they send their prayers to Jesus Christ who in turn sends their requests to God the Father.[7] Christ is taken to be a mediator par excellence because he is very close to God. As the Son of God and because he also experienced our humanity, he knows our needs better than anyone else and speaks to God the Father on our behalf more effectively than any other ancestor. He is able to express our needs to God in the best way possible. Christ is like an ancestor because he was truly human. At his birth in Bethlehem, Christ became a real living being. He took human flesh and his actions became like those of an ordinary man such as eating, sleeping, drinking, crying and getting tired. After his death he ascended to heaven to become our representative in God's seat where he intercedes on our behalf.[8]

In this context, it appears, in order to make Christ meaningful and relevant to Tswana, African Independent Churches have formulated an ancestor-based christology whereby Christ is considered as the greatest of the ancestors standing at the apex of the hierarchy of the ancestral spirits. The intermediary role of Christ is not just one among many but the fulfilment or the consummation of the intermediary role of all the ancestors. In this regard, when prayers are uttered to God during church services they are, quite often, said in the

7 Int. Archbishop George Gojamu, Holy Sarda Church, Mmathethe, 19.10.1991.
8 Int. M.L. Dikgang, Christian Brethren Assembly Church, Serowe, 18.12.1991.

name of the ancestors and Christ who is seated at the right hand of God as the intercessor and intermediary of the people here on earth.

(b) Healer

Another common christological title of Jesus is that of *Ngaka* (Healer). Because of his powers to heal all kinds of sickness, as observed in the records of the New Testament, nearly all African Independent Churches believe and teach that Jesus is a great physician.

It is also believed that the healing power of Jesus is inherent in the church today and can be exercised by the prophet-healers, bishops, elders of the Church and the entire congregation which is the body of Christ. Therefore Christ, who is present in the Church today, heals through the worshipping activities of the church today. He heals those who suffer spiritually, physically, mentally and socially. In the prayers of healing, the power of Jesus heals people and also comforts those who suffer from various calamities or disasters in life by the power of the Holy Spirit.[9]

The love of God for his people is seen more clearly in the healing miracles of Jesus and his power to raise the dead. This being the case healing has been a centre of attraction in the life and work of many African Independent Churches. To this end the Person of Christ is conceived as the healing hand of God the Healer par excellence. Jesus came into the world to teach and show people how much God loves them. This he did through his healing activities which were done with great mercy and compassion, thus displaying God's love at its best. On the basis of this theological understanding, members of the African Independent Churches strive to heal one another the best they can as a continuation of Christ's ministry of healing.

2. Pneumatology

It is important to point out that the Holy Spirit is the life blood of the African Independent Churches and because of their emphasis on the role that the Holy Spirit plays in the life of the church the Independent Churches in Botswana are commonly known as "Spiritual Churches". Their understanding of the nature and work of the Holy Spirit, however, is still a matter of great debate. Oost-

9 Oosthuizen, *Post-Christianity*, pp. 120-122.

huizen has argued that there is a misunderstanding of the person and work of the Holy Spirit in what he calls the nativistic movements. According to Oosthuizen, there is a confusion regarding the relationship between the ancestral spirits and the Holy Spirit. It is maintained that there is a close connection between the Holy Spirit and the ancestors in the Independent Churches. For instance, instruction from the Spirit may lead to the acquisition of two, three or more wives, in which case the Spirit's activity is not related to moral guidance but rather to vital force. Pauw, cited in Oosthuizen, has indicated that the belief in the Holy Spirit does not completely displace the belief in ancestors in Zulu Zionist Churches. Oosthuizen has seriously questioned the orthodox nature of the concept of the Holy Spirit in African Independent Churches. In his estimation the doctrine of the Spirit in the Independent Churches is the wide gate through which a number of pre-Christian conceptions have entered into Christianity. "The Spirit", he writes, "is the channel through which the ancestral ideas enter Christian conceptions, with the result that something different is practiced".[10] Sometimes, it is pointed out, church leaders claim to possess the Holy Spirit in such a way that he becomes the monopoly of the leaders, it is actually at their disposal, as in the case of the ancestors who can be ceremoniously scolded if they do not react favourably after sacrifices have been offered to them.[11] It has further been noted that the functions of the ancestral spirits in the African Independent Churches have been transferred to the Holy Spirit or simply the "Spirit" so that in the independent post-Christian movements their Holy Spirit is no longer the Holy Spirit of whom we learn in Scripture.[12] Furthermore, the fact that a distinction is made between God the Father and the Holy Spirit, in the sense that they are not co-equal and co-eternal as confessed in the Athanasian Creed, has led people such as Oosthuizen to conclude that the doctrine of the Spirit in the new churches leaves much to be desired. Despite some obvious misunderstandings regarding the nature of the Holy Spirit, the Third Person of the Holy Trinity plays a very important and significant role in the life and work of the African Independent Churches. Like Jesus Christ, the Holy Spirit is considered as a Healer and Mediator. By and large, he is considered as the healing agent acting through the human activities of the prophet-healer, Bishop, any individual Christian or the whole congre-

10 *Ibid.*, p. 123.
11 *Ibid.*, p. 124.
12 *Ibid.*, p. 125.

gation in the Church. The Holy Spirit helps prophets and healers in their work of healing the sick. His work is to provide the healing power. He is present in the Church to heal the wounds of the sinful humanity. He gives the healers, prophets and bishops wisdom and knowledge to diagnose diseases. Through the Holy Spirit, they know the causes of diseases when patients come to them for healing and helps them to prescribe the effective medicine for their diseases.[13]

3. Soteriology

Daneel has contrasted the missionary approach to salvation with that found in the African Independent Churches and found the former lacking in its impact. Daneel puts it thus:

> The missionary readily proclaimed a gospel of the soul's salvation, but appeared to be silent on issues of politics, man's physical needs and his daily struggle for survival. Looking at it from the holistic African point of view this moralistic gospel did not spell out convincingly the salvation of the entire man. It was insufficiently related to the perplexities caused by illness and misfortune. Neither did it seem to hold much hope for liberation from oppressive colonial structures, within which Africans found themselves and which missionaries appeared to represent and even perpetuate.[14]

According to Daneel, the communication of Good News in the African Independent Churches is overwhelmingly appealing to the Africans because of its holistic nature and because of its dynamism and relatedness to the African world view and specifically African needs in all spheres of life.[15] It should be noted that in their understanding of salvation, the Independent churches consider the whole person is in need of salvation. This includes the soul as well as the body.

Apart from the missionary oriented view of salvation, African Independent Churches go beyond the mere understanding that the souls of human beings need salvation from Christ. They also advocate that salvation is much wider

---

[13] Int. Bishop Abisolome Seema and K.P. Tsumake, Galatia Church in Zion, Mogonye, 24.11.91.
[14] M.L. Daneel, "The Missionary Outreach of African Independent Churches", *Missionalia*, vol. 8, no. 3, 1980, p. 58.
[15] Ibid., p. 58.

than what missionary christianity perceives it to be. Without physical emancipation, people cannot attain the fullness of life because their bodies are still enslaved in physical hardships. In most cases, it is believed, spiritual sickness affects the proper functioning of the body and the proper functioning of the soul. In order to attain the fullness of life, therefore, human beings need salvation in its totality. This includes salvation from epidemics, diseases of all kinds, drought, barrenness, famine, fear of the unknown, jealousies, witchcraft, poverty, colonial oppression, social discrimination, loneliness and death. It is in this context that Independent Churches in Botswana have managed to attract many people into their rank and file, because they cater for almost every aspect of human need as Jesus did during his earthly ministry in Palestine.

It is important to note that on this account, although African Independent Churches emphatically preach about heaven, they also emphasize the importance of experiencing salvation here on earth by alleviating human suffering that people experience every day. This stands in sharp contrast with the mission churches where church leaders are reluctant to address the needs of their congregations holistically.

4. Ecclesiology

Another important innovation that African Independent Churches have brought into the doctrine of the church in Botswana is their understanding that the church cannot be limited to the believers whose names appear in the registry of the church. The church does not exist in isolation. It exists in the community and the community comprises those who are alive here and now, those yet to be born and those who are dead and gone to their resting places, the living dead. David Barrett has it that the concept of salvation of the African Independent Churches entails the view that salvation is only found in community in which case the ancestors can be considered as participating members of the ongoing brotherhood.[16]

Although it is generally understood by African Independent Church members that the church is a new community comprising those who have believed and been baptized in the name of Jesus Christ, it is also understood that it does

---

16 David Barrett, *Schism and Renewal in Africa*, Nairobi: OUP, 1968, p. 169.

not constitute a total break with the African community at large. In some instances, therefore, it is believed that the ancestral spirits who constitute the church triumphant, are an extension of the militant church on earth without whom the church is inconceivable. This concept of the church emphasizes the indissolubility of the relationships between the living and the living-dead. The church finds its meaning in the life of its members on the fact that it is a community of believers comprising those living here and now, the ancestors and those yet to be born.

It is interesting to note that this idea of the *ecclesia* consisting not only of the living but also of the living dead is not peculiar to African Independent Churches in Botswana. It seems to be fairly common in a number of indigenous churches across Africa. A typical example of the extent in which the ancestors can be considered as an extension of the church militant is drawn from the names given to some of these churches. For example, the Herero Church, which was formed in Namibia in 1955, is commonly known as "Oruuano", which simply means the community, thereby implying that even the ancestors are part and parcel of the new community of believers and that their participation is not only desirable but necessary as guardians of the people and mediators between the people and the Living God.[17]

5. Worship

Another area of theological significance where indigenization is currently taking place is the area of worship. Here, like many other areas of Christian life, African Independent Churches in Botswana have introduced certain African elements that make Christian worship truly indigenous to Tswana. Their Africanness has attracted a great deal of worshippers who through these churches satisfy their emotional needs before God their Creator. Akin Omoyajowo, writing about the nature of worship in the mission churches, has noted that their liturgies have failed to attract many African peoples because of their foreignness. Omoyajowo puts it thus:

> The liturgies of the Western-established churches .... were all imported from the traditions of their home missions. This is why services of worship in them are lifeless, drab, boring and un-inspiring. The liturgies

[17] P. Pollitzer, "Ancestor Veneration in the Oruuano Movement", *Missionalia*, vol. 12, no. 3, p. 124-128.

> become stereotyped, formal, monotonous and absolutely unrelated to the African way of worship. The simple reason for this awful situation is that they were not composed from the spiritual, emotional and ritual needs of the people and so they have remained essentially alien to Africans.[18]

The Worship of God in the African Independent Churches is deeply spiritual and emotional. Their liturgies are informal, relaxed, exciting, and full of symbolic actions and words. They are intended to satisfy the emotional and spiritual needs of their members. There is great congregational participation, with the pastors only providing some form of direction and a sense of order. Omoyajowo has indicated that this is typical of the African peoples. When it comes to worship they want to be fully involved in uttering praises to God and not to be mere spectators. Omoyajowo puts it this way:

> The African wants to be actively involved in the worship of the deity. He is not content with being a passive spectator; he wants to be a dynamic participant .... The indigenous churches are characterized by a great measure of spontaneity and excitability. Their use of indigenous music is an innovation which accounts for much of their evangelistic achievements. Africans naturally love rhythm, they love to sing in a way that is meaningful to them. All these means have been employed by the indigenous churches to bring Christianity home to the African within his cultural setting.[19]

Generally speaking, worship in African Independent Churches is essentially ritualistic in a sense that it is full of symbols pregnant with religious meaning. One of the dominant factors in worship is singing. African tunes are used to enable all the participants to sing and enjoy themselves in praising the Lord. By and large, singing is accompanied by clapping of hands, ringing of bells, trumpeting, heavy drumming and most important of all dancing. African Independent Churches use Psalm 150 as the theological justification for using musical instruments in the church such as drums, trumpets, bells, gongs as well as dancing during worship. They also make reference to David who danced before the Ark of the Lord, as recorded in 2 Samuel 6:12-16. Adrian Hastings, in his critique of the mission churches' failure to meet the ritual needs of the African people, has this to say:

---

18 Omoyajowo, "An African Expression of Christianity", p. 66.
19 Ibid., p. 66.

> In the field of ritual too .... Protestant missionary life offered little else than a void to replace the intricate network of ritual and sacrifice and protective amulet of traditional religion - a whole complex symbolic structure of rite, the use of space and time, of colour and particular objects, which had been so central to the previous religious experience of most Africans .... The quest of the Independent Church was the quest for a ritual, a belief, and a realized community in and through which immediate human needs, social, psychological and physical could be appropriately met. Too many such needs had hardly been met at all in a meaningful way by the mission churches.[20]

Dancing, perhaps more than anything else, gives the new churches one of their distinctive African characteristics, for dancing before God and the ancestors has always been the chief characteristic of African worship throughout the African continent. It is interesting to note that one of the outcomes of dancing during worship in the African Independent Churches is possession by the Holy Spirit. In the Holy Galilee Church it is held that spirit possession by the Holy Spirit enables members of the church to speak in tongues, heal the sick, and to utter prophetic messages for the congregation and the community at large. Members of the church speak in tongues during worship as a sign that the Holy Spirit has descended upon them.[21] In most cases when members of the church are possessed by the Holy Spirit, they speak in strange tongues such as Xhosa, Ndebele, English and Sotho.[22]

6. Ancestors

Because of their key position in African societies, attacks on the ancestors by missionaries in the missionary field became one of the factors that gave rise to church independence. This was the case among the Herero in Namibia. According to Philip Pollitzer, one of the reasons that led to the formation of the Okereka Jevangeli Joruuano (Oruuano), popularly known as the Herero Church in 1955, was the desire by the Herero to venerate their ancestors freely. The white missionaries rejected ancestor veneration as practiced among the Herero. The Herero suspected that this rejection was done not only on

---

20 Adrian Hastings, *A History of African Christianity 1895-1954*, **Cambridge**: Cambridge University Press, 1976, pp. 712.

21 Int. Bishop J. Abeng, Holy Galilee Church, Gaborone, 4.1.91.

22 Int. Archbishop B.S. Tumagole, Dipesalema Church, 3.4.91.

religious grounds but also because the whites wanted to deprive them of their nationhood.[23]

In many African societies, ancestors are concerned with the fertility of their descendants, the fertility of the soil and the availability of good weather upon which the other two are dependent. Because of their close association with the living and their proximity to God, the ancestral spirits are considered as intermediaries between God and man. David Barrett in his study of African societies has noted that the belief in ancestral spirits is predominant in almost all African societies mainly as an expression of family and clan continuity and solidarity. The recently deceased ancestors are quite often regarded as still inhabiting the family land. They exercise control over the living and all life exists under their surveillance. Barrett observed that the ancestors are treated with awe, fear, reverence, respect and veneration and their influence penetrates in almost every sphere of life.[24] According to Barrett, the resilience of the belief in ancestors is based on the fact that

> Among the Bantu race in particular it represents the hierarchical social system carried over into the spirit world; it validates the traditional political structure; it ensures fertility, health, prosperity and the continuity of past and future in family life; it is a sanction for the respect of living elders. To attack it, therefore was to attack the very foundations of tribal and family structure.[25]

Because of their importance and significance in almost all African societies, the ancestors have been accommodated in most African Independent Churches in varying degrees. Kofi Appiah-Kubi, writing about the role of the ancestors in the Indigenous Churches in Ghana, has this to say:

> Another important area of attraction is the importance these churches place on veneration of ancestors, who are said to be the custodians of law, morality and ethical order of the Akan. The mission churches, while overlooking the Akan ancestors, urge their members to venerate St George of England, St Andrew of Scotland or St Christopher of the Vatican, who are very much removed from the convert's daily wants and anxieties.[26]

---

23 Pollitzer, "Ancestor Veneration", p. 124.
24 Barrett, *Schism and Renewal*, p. 119.
25 *Ibid.*, p. 119.
26 Appiah-Kubi, "Indigenous Christian Churches", p. 120.

In the context of Botswana, it appears, a number of African Independent churches allow and encourage their members to pray to God through their ancestors in accordance with their culture. It is argued that Christ, as a Jew, prayed to his father mentioning the names of Abraham, Isaac and Jacob, his ancestors according to Jewish culture.[27] According to the Nazareth Church of Botswana, belief in ancestral spirits persists in many churches because Jesus said that he came not to destroy the traditions of the people but to fulfil them (Mt 5:17).[28] By and large a number of the African Independent Churches believe in the saving powers of the ancestors. Ancestral spirits appear in dreams and visions. It is generally believed that this shows the immortality of man, thereby assuring us that there is life after death.

Quite often, a number of churches make offerings to the ancestral spirits asking them to take prayers of the people to God so that he can help them. A considerable number of leaders of the new churches argue that before the church came to Botswana, Tswana had a strong belief in their ancestral spirits who acted as intermediaries between them and God. The arrival of the Bible did not abrogate the role of the ancestors as intermediaries but provided an additional channel of communication with God. Because of this, their role as intercessors still continues.[29] The majority of African Independent Churches in Botswana believe that it is wrong that early missionaries tried hard to persuade the African people to reject their ancestors. Ancestors are an effective means of communication between God as a spiritual being and man. One function of the ancestral spirits is to guide members of the church in times of conflict by warning them before hand through dreams of the impending dangers and how to overcome them.[30] In some churches the saving assistance of the ancestral spirits is sought on a daily basis. For example, in St Mark's Service Church, the ancestral spirits are prayed to daily in the mornings and evenings asking them to help the church to heal the sick and also in times of drought. Appeals are made to the ancestral spirits by means of offerings and sacrifices. Animals or a drinking party using local traditional beer and snuff are offered to them because the ancestors used to like these things.[31] Certain

---

27 Int. Pastor Keletso Keana, Ezekiel Church of Botswana, Selebi-Phikwe, 12.91.
28 Int. Bishop B. Bolokwe, Nazareth Church, Ramotswa, 16.7.91.
29 Int. Bishop Sacks Masaka Chakaloba, Jesus Look Intently Church, Tonota, 5.1.91.
30 Int. Bishop J.R. Mokgele, St Isaac's Church in Salvation, Mochudi, 15.9.91.
31 Int. Archbishop Julius Mpofu, St Mark's Service Church, Tati Siding, 3.7.92.

African Independent Churches recognize the intercessory power of the ancestral spirits especially in connection with rain making ceremonies. This is specially so among the Kalanga where some African Independent Churches associate themselves with the Mwari Cult. For example the Messiah Church of Ten Commandments maintains close ties with the Mwari Cult at Ramokgwebana. Whenever need arises, members of the church and followers of the Mwari cult pray together at the mountain of Mwari for rain.[32]

7. Rites of passage

Rites of passage constitute one of the foundation stones of African religions. Their main purpose is to create and maintain fixed and meaningful transformations in the life-cycle of the individual from birth, through to puberty, marriage and death. Ceremonies that are associated with rites of passage have three major elements, namely separation, transition and incorporation. Such ceremonies provide the occasion when the individual crosses over from the sphere of everyday mundane experiences into the sphere of the sacred, thereby being spiritually transformed and incorporated into another social reality.

(a) Birth rites

One of these has to do with birth rites. For instance, in the Botswana Crusaders Church, seven days after the birth of a child the Bishop prepares *sewacho* which is used to protect the child against witchcraft. He applies it all over the body of the baby while prayers are being said. Then the Bishop or pastor takes some wool and ties it round the waist and the neck of the child. Some oil is put on fire and the child inhales the smoke to protect him/her against all kinds of dangers or evil powers.[33] Another example can be drawn from the Botswana Melkzetive Church. According to this church, seven days after the birth of a baby boy or 14 days after the birth of a baby girl, church women pray for the child at home. They put incense on fire and make the child inhale the smoke. Water is blessed and the child is given a ritual bath to protect him/her from evil powers.[34] In some cases the symbol of the cross is used as a means of protecting newly born children. This is the case in the Christian

---

32 Int. Pastor Christopher Phambuka, Messiah Church of Ten Commandments, Gaborone, 9.11.91.

33 Int. Bishop Steve Mokwena, Botswana Crusaders Church, Francistown, 3.1.91.

34 Int. Bishop Amos Makhani, Botswana Melkzetive Church, Francistown, 1.8.92.

Brethren Church and the Heaven Apostolic Church. In these churches, after the birth of a child, the baby is smeared with *sewacho* on the head in the form of a cross around the neck and the umbilical cord by a bishop or pastor.

Sometimes *sewacho* of cow dung is applied in a form of a circle at the back of the head. This ritual protects and strengthens the baby against witchcraft, jealousies, other children and moral impurities emanating from other people in the community who may come in contact with the child. This ensures healthy growth of the body, mind and spirit. The ceremony takes place 14 days after the birth of the child.[35] Mention should also be made here of the naming ceremony of a newly born baby in some of the new churches. The Morian Episcopal Church in Zion offers a good example of how a Christian rite has been contextualized. Prior to the naming ceremony, prayers are held throughout the night during which people read portions from scripture and preach. A debate is held by the congregation calling the child with different names. During the time of naming the child, the Pastor reads Luke 1:62 and hands over a piece of paper to the father to write the name of the child. But instead of writing it, the father gives the name verbally. The congregation makes a loud murmur of surprise when they hear the name as recorded in the Bible.[36]

8. Marriage

Marriage has been an area of great conflict in the missionary field since the Christian Church was planted in Africa. David Barrett has indicated that polygamy has always been a normal and sanctioned institution in a number of African societies. In a number of cases "polygamy has been a necessary element in the economy, a matter of prestige for men, a guarantee of security for women and a foundation of family, clan and tribe".[37] In many African Independent Churches polygamous marriages are tolerated though they may not be officially sanctioned.

Oosthuizen has noted that "among the Tswana, while the established churches oppose polygamy, the independent church movements are quite favourably disposed to it .... and monogamy is frequently regarded not as a

35 Int. M.L. Dikgang, Christian Brethren Assembly Church, Serowe, 18.12.91; Bishop April Ethokeng Sidimo, Heaven Apostolic Church, 19.12.91.

36 Int. Sir Wonder, Gaborone, 19.1.96.

37 Barrett, *Schism and Renewal*, p. 116.

Christian institution so much as a specifically European one, lacking scriptural sanction".[38] In Botswana African Independent Churches adhere to the Biblical view of marriage as a sacred institution ordained by God as recorded in Gen 1:27-30 and 2:7, 21-24. It is generally understood that marriage is supposed to be a life-long, one-flesh union between husband and wife for the purposes of procreation, companionship, rearing of children and inheritance of property. The majority of the new churches accept monogamy as an ideal form of marriage. However, monogamy is not taken to be the only form of marriage for Christians. In some churches, for example, polygamy is practiced openly in accordance with Tswana marriage traditions. Such churches maintain that since polygamous marriages are allowed in Tswana society, especially in cases of childlessness, they do not constitute a sin against God because it is the will of God that a married couple must have children in fulfilment of the command "be fruitful and multiply and fill the earth and subdue it"(Gen 1: 28).

Besides, Independent Churches which practice polygamy base their theological arguments on the polygamous nature of marriage in the Old Testament. It has been observed that plural marriages were sanctioned in the Old Testament and the law of Deuteronomy did not forbid them (Deut 21:15-17). In the time of the Old Testament, large families were desirable and on this account polygamy, concubines, handmaids and secondary wives were common place. Both during the time of the patriarchs and the kings, polygamy was considered normal practice. The earliest example of polygamy was the marriage of Lamech to Adah and Zillah (Gen 4:19). There are other examples in the Old Testament of men who were polygamous, some of whom found great favour in the sight of God. These included people such as Abraham (Gen 16:15), Esau (Gen 26:25; 28:9), Jacob (Gen 29:16-30; 30:3-9) and Elkana (1 Sam 1:2). Among the kings, David, a man after God's own heart (1 Sam 18:27; 2 Sam 5:13-16; 11:15,27) and Solomon (1 Kin 11:3) had the reputation of having several wives. At the time of Moses polygamy was legislated as a social and legal institution.

On the basis of the reasons given above, several churches in Botswana practice polygamy. Few of these need special mention here. In the first instance in churches such as Africa Gospel Church, Gospel of God Church and Johane Church of God, men are allowed to marry as many wives as they want depending on their income. Polygamous marriages are allowed within

---

38 Oosthuizen, *Post-Christianity*, pp. 181.

the church between men and women but not between members of the same sex. Polyandry is not allowed because it is conceived as immoral since it is against God's order of creation.[39]

9. Healing

One of the most distinctive features of the African Independent Churches in Botswana is their reputation to heal people suffering from all manner of diseases. Healing forms the central part of their religious activities. The theological basis of their healing ministry is a belief in a healing God whose healing activities are recorded in the Bible both in the Old and New Testaments. In the Old Testament, God the Creator is conceived as a Healer. In the Old Testament there is the story of Namaan the Syrian army commander who suffered from leprosy and was healed by prophet Elisha as recorded in 2 Kings 5:1-14. On the basis of the teaching of the Bible, African Independent Churches have become hospitals where spiritual healing takes place. Adrian Hastings writing about the phenomenon of healing in the new churches, puts it thus:

> Prayers for healing became the central activity of the Spiritual Churches in most of West, Central and Southern Africa. While the missionary approach of scientific medicine was only partly rejected, it had reached far too few people and excluded too many problems to fulfil the needs of the common man. Rituals of healing were among the most important of those in traditional society, and the most characteristic motivation of the new Christian movements in Africa .... (*was*) the establishment of accessible rites of healing with a Christian reference and with a caring community by gifted and spiritual individuals claiming an initiative effectively denied them in the older churches.[40]

One very important aspect of the theology of healing in the African Independent Churches is their acceptance and use of African traditional medicine in the church. By and large the use of traditional medicine is not condoned in the main-line churches and although members of the mission churches do visit traditional doctors, they do so without the official approval of their churches. This is not the case in the African Independent Churches. The new churches

---

39 Int. Pastor J. Mpofu, Gospel of God Church, 25.2.91.

40 Hastings, *A History of African Christianity* 1950-1975, Cambridge: CUP, 1979, p. 72.

consider Tswana traditional medicine as a gift from God in order to save human life. Life is conceived as the ultimate blessing from God and on that account it must be safeguarded by all means available, including the use of traditional medicine. It is commonly believed that the knowledge of such traditional medicines and their use comes from God through the ancestral spirits and, to some extent, through the Holy Spirit who inspires the prophet-healers. Omoyajowo writes:

> The whole point of divine healing is an answer to one of the problems which drive the believer back to the traditional religion. The role of the healer is similar to that of the traditional healer .... The traditional causes of illness are accepted by the indigenous churches especially those that can be attributed to the malignant spiritual powers, witches and implacable enemies.[41]

Daneel has indicated that there are striking similarities between faith healing and traditional healing. The diagnosis of the prophetic healer quite often resembles that of the traditional medicine man in that both of them concentrate on the personal causes of the sickness or mishap. If the sick person's condition is not caused by a living enemy making use of magic, it is attributable to an evil, alien or ancestral spirit.[42] The prophet healer explains the Christian message to the patient at a vital personal level of existence. By taking seriously the patient's traditional experience of threat to his or her life and their need for protection, he effects a confrontation between the besetting evil power and the liberating power of the Christian God.[43] The most characteristic element in faith healing as against traditional healing is that:

> through the prophet healer the Spirit himself reveals the cause and nature of the disease or temptation and prescribes the required therapy. Through the power of the Holy Spirit as expressed in prophetic exorcism the evil powers are expelled and protection against future threats is obtained. In all this the prophet healer is the key figure.[44]

In a number of African Independent Churches diagnosis of ailments is done by divination through the Bible. Traditionally this is done by means of throwing

---

41 Omoyajowo, "An African Expression of Christianity", p. 67.
42 Daneel, *Quest for Belonging*, p. 239.
43 *Ibid.*, p. 239.
44 *Ibid.*

bones by the diviner as a means of gaining knowledge regarding the cause of a particular disease. In the Independent Churches this has been replaced by the Bible. It seems that the continuation of divination in the new churches by the use of the Bible, attracts many people to these churches because they provided a link between their own traditional way of diagnosing disease and the church. In this way the church is identified with the people who look at it no longer as a foreign institution, but as part of their religious heritage, meeting their needs as they feel them fit. As a matter of fact the prophet healer, by engaging himself in divination with the help of the Bible, replaces the traditional healer in a manner that is satisfying to the Christian believer. Akin Omoyajowo puts it this way:

> But with the emergence of African Independent Churches, he finds a most effective substitute for the traditional diviner in their prophets. Their roles are fundamentally identical. Here the suppliant finds a church ministering to his spiritual and existential needs. It is no longer that alien church which failed to see eye to eye with him. As was the case with the diviner, he is given concrete objects to aid his prayer and restore his confidence holy water, candles, incense, consecrated oil, psalms to rehearse, Bible passages to recite. No longer does he need to go to a diviner. Jesus Christ has proved that his faith can be given expression from the perspective of his tradition and culture.[45]

For instance, in the Ezekiel Church of Botswana each branch has a special Bible which has already been prayed for by the Bishop and set aside for healing ceremonies. When a patient comes he or she is given the Bible to open. Once opened the Holy Spirit inspires the prophets and reveals to them the cause of the illness and the necessary treatment for a given disease.[46] In other churches the Bishop or Prophet-healer holds the Bible and prays to God on behalf of the sick. He then opens the Bible and reads wherever he has opened. As he reads the passage in the Bible the Holy Spirit reveals to him the nature of the disease of the patient and its cause. The Holy Spirit also reveals to the prophet-healer the type of treatment required for that kind of disease.[47]

---

45 *Ibid.*

46 Int. Keletso Keana, Ezekiel Church or Botswana, 9.12.91.

47 Int. Bishop J. Abeng, Holy Galilee Church, Gaborone, 4.2.92.

Concluding Remarks

In this paper I have argued that since its inception in Africa, Christianity has failed to Africanize itself fast enough and deep enough to make Christianity indigenous in Africa as it is indigenous in Europe and America. The missionary approach was suspicious of local beliefs, values and practices and in this account, Gospel and culture were perceived as antagonistic to each other. The early African theologians such as Tertullian, Augustine of Hippo, St Cyprian and others made no attempt to Africanize the church since they were catering for the spiritual needs of the Roman and Greek middle classes that constituted the African Church in north Africa. The failure to contextualize the church in Africa became more and more noticeable during the missionary era when the missionary approach called for the total eradication of African culture. It has been argued in this paper that as the Gospel spread far and wide in Africa, many Africans began to recognize the relevance of Christianity in their lives. Some of them formed their own independent churches and began to look for ways and means of explaining the gospel to their fellow Africans in the way in which they could understand. This they did by employing African culture to explain a whole range of the doctrines of the church.

It is generally acknowledged today that African Independent Churches are already producing a relevant theology for Africans by expressing their Christianity in African cultural terms. This includes their understanding of the person and work of Christ, the Holy Spirit, salvation, the nature of the Church, worship, healing and others. They also include in their belief systems and Christian living a place for the ancestors, divination, prophecy, sacrifices, plural marriages and a number of other African cultural aspects without necessarily compromising the Gospel. In this way African Independent Churches have attracted many African people into their fold. It can thus be seen that while we are still searching for a theology cooked in an African pot, African Independent Churches have already cooked one which is relevant to the African people here and now.

Christology in the Inculturated Shona Burial Ritual in the Roman Catholic Church in Zimbabwe

Paul H. Gundani

One problem that Shona Catholics continue to face is to make a smooth transition from an ancestor-based world-view to the Christian trinitarian monotheism. While both Shona religion and Catholicism thrive on mediatory agents, the authority vested in the mediators and the jurisdiction for which such authority is to be understood makes the programme of inculturation[1] of the Catholic faith a rather interesting but complex area of study.

This article focuses on the area of inculturation of the Shona Catholic burial rite with the objective of investigating the place given to Christ.

Historical Background

The burial rite that is discussed below came about as a result of the changing ecclesiological, liturgical and "political" changes in global, as well as local Catholicism. Two notable but mutually related factors behind the formulation of the rite include the reform espoused by the Second Vatican Council, at a global level, and the call for radical liturgical changes by indigenous priests in the early 60's, at the local level. While the latter can be understood as a response to the former, it is important to see the response to the teachings of Vatican II by local clergy, as having taken a decidedly different direction from that of missionary clergy. This point will become clearer later.

(i) Vatican II's impact on liturgical developments

Early missionary practice had been characterized by substituting the traditional African rites by a Mass. Consequently, Shona customs associated

---

1 Inculturation is according to Aylward Shorter, "the creative and dynamic relationship between the Christian message and culture or cultures" (Aylward Shorter, *Towards a Theology of Inculturation*, Maryknoll: Orbis, 1988, p. 11).

with death and burial were sidelined, and so were those associated with respect for the ancestors.[2]

With respect to burial, Catholic missionaries believed that a Requiem Mass replete with ceremony and ritual would equal the customary Shona practice. They also believed that 'approved' Catholic burial practices were complete and adequate so as to eradicate the need to propitiate the ancestors and to integrate the 'departed ones' into the whole family.[3] However, no matter how the missionary Church called upon their flock to abandon the traditional practices, the latter persisted besides "Christian" practice and rites.

Vatican II's call for greater adaptation in the field of liturgy provided impetus and breathing space for creative experiments with new rites. Dachs and Rea rightly argue that after Vatican II the Catholic hierarchy in Zimbabwe was under pressure "to reassess their attitudes to African social custom". The question of burial was among the first to be considered.

(ii) Indigenisation of the Priesthood

Apart from Vatican II's call for the reform of the liturgy, there was another driving force for change among Shona Catholics. Calls for local vocation to priesthood and sisterhood[4] yielded a substantial increase in indigenous personnel which in turn provided an added impetus for an adjustment of ritual and liturgy to "closer conformity with African social custom and habit in order to make the local Church more appreciably African than Western European".[5] One of the champions for liturgical change was the late Joseph Kumbirai who later left the priesthood. By early 1966 (just after the Council was concluded) Kumbirai had already formulated a burial rite which, he argued, was capable of meeting the spiritual needs of Shona Catholics. He had already tried it in the Salisbury and Gweru dioceses and was receiving applause. He thus warned the Bishops of Rhodesia (now Zimbabwe):

> In Africa we have to face the problem of either building a liturgy almost from the ground up or of transplanting a European liturgical

---

2 A.J. Dachs and W.F. Rea, *The Catholic Church and Zimbabwe (1879-1979)*, Gweru: Mambo, 1979, pp. 223f.

3 *Ibid.*, p. 224.

4 *Ibid.*, p. 245.

5 *Ibid.*, p. 223.

> structure and then start chopping off and adding and patching up until we end with something neither African nor European.[6]

In Kumbirai's opinion, the only way forward was to produce a new rite, one which was "typically African".[7] By this he meant a rite that was "in a Shona cast, based on customs and traditions of the of the Shona"[8] In the proposed rite, Kumbirai also insisted on the need for a *kususukidza* prayer where the dead ancestors are asked by the living to take their child to God.[9]

The spirit of reform spurred by Vatican II as well as the calls for radical adaptation coming from indigenous clergy of the likes of Kumbirai caught up with the nationalistic zeal of the 1960's which promoted the quest for African authenticity in all areas having to do with culture.[10]

In response to the pressure referred to above, in September 1966, the Bishops of Rhodesia, after carefully considering the arguments in favour of reform, set up a Committee to prepare a draft of the Shona burial rite in Christian form.[11] Kumbirai was one of the key members of the committee, and not surprisingly his experimental rite provided the backbone to the draft that the Committee presented to the Bishops' conference.[12] On receiving the draft rite, the Bishops in turn sent it to an Interdiocesan Liturgical Commission for vetting. Finally on 28 September 1966, at Gweru, the Inter-diocesan Liturgical Commission approved the proposed rite of burial. The Commission subsequently presented the rite to the Bishops' Conference who, at the end of 1966, approved it *ad experimentum* for three years. Henceforth, a Christianized Shona burial rite, *Maitiro okuvipa Munhu*, *was* presented for use to Shona Catholics in Zimbabwe.[13] Although the rite has been amended twice since 1966, it has basically remained the same in intent and purpose. It is this rite that we will analyse in order to determine its Christological character.

---

6 Driefontein Mission Archives, Kumbirai to Bishops (Gweru, 25.1.1966); cf. Dachs and Rea, *The Catholic Church and Zimbabwe*.

7 *Ibid.*

8 *Ibid.*

9 *Ibid.*

10 Dachs and Rea, *The Catholic Church and Zimbabwe*, p. 223.

11 Rhodesia Catholic Bishops Conference minutes, Gen. Sec. File p. 10.

12 Fr Mavhudzi (Int. 16.11.1996) was a member of this committee but was against Kumbirai's radical approach.

13 General Secretariat Archives, IBM file (p. 8). Cf. Bishop A. Haene, President of the Inter-diocesan Liturgical Commission's report to the Bishops' Conference.

Rites Performed Immediately after the Death of a Catholic

When someone dies among the Shona he/she is taken home to lie in state in the main family hut/house. The main family hut/house is the appropriate place at which funeral rituals can begin to be performed. Furthermore, it is the central sacred place where the family members, relatives and friends, in a show of solidarity, come to pay their last respects to the deceased. As for the deceased it is an honour to be afforded the chance to bid farewell to family and friends before embarking on a journey which may lead to the world of the ancestors (*Nyikadzimu*).

From the time of entry into the hut/house, family members, especially women relatives and friends mourn the dead, sing songs, dance, read the scriptures and pray. They keep the deceased company and never leave him/her unattended. Outside the hut/house male relatives and friends keep a vigil throughout the night.

At about midmorning, the process towards burial begins. However, before "accompanying" the deceased to the grave, family members and friends are called into the hut/house to bid farewell to the deceased. At this juncture, an appointed elder or priest or catechist is asked to make a (ritual) prayer to the ancestors of the deceased, informing them of the death of their grandson or grand-daughter. While in customary practice the one to lead the prayer was invariably the senior member of the family, within the context of the Church, it is recommended that a senior Catholic family member lead the prayers.[14] The prayer recommended by the Catholic Church goes as is stated below.[15]

1. Prayer to the ancestors

Leader:

To you all ancestors who are with God. We are gathered here to present to you your child x. We ask you to accompany him/her on his/her journey. Receive him/her in God's kingdom so that he/she will have the capacity to shield others from the misfortunes of the world and to intercede on their

---

14 Zimbabwe Catholic Bishops' Conference (ZCBC), *Maitiro Okuviga Munhu* (Order for Burial), Gweru: Mambo, rev. ed., 1989 [1967], p. 30.

15 All prayers quoted in this essay have been translated from Shona to English by the author.

behalf. May you lead him/her to the joys and happiness of the righteous. where he/she will live for ever more.

Response: *Amen.*[16]

Following the prayer to the ancestors, pall-bearers are instructed to carry the hearse out of the hut/house. Immediately after exiting, the pall-bearers are asked to place it down. At this moment the leader (same as in the prayer above) leads in another prayer, directed to God:

2. Prayer to God to welcome the deceased

Leader:

Brethren, we have assembled here to pray for our brother/sister x who has left us. Let us pray in earnest that God may welcome him/her in his kingdom. In the name of the Father and of the Son and of the Holy Spirit.

Response: *Amen.*

Pause

Leader: *Glory be to God*
Response: *For ever and ever*
Leader: *Lord hear our prayers*
Response: *Hear us Lord*
Leader: *Let us pray*

God of heaven and earth, the merciful one, we your children are assembled here to accompany your child x who has left us. You are the one who has called him/her away from us. Let there be no other abode for him/her except where you are. Receive him/her. You are his/her owner .... May you forgive him/her all the sins that he/she committed against you and lead him/her on to the place of happiness and joy. Have mercy on him/her; do not judge him/her harshly .... Father, receive your child in your abode where he/she will live happily ever after with all the saints, his/her paternal and maternal ancestors and relatives who are with you. Christ our Lord, convey our prayers to God the Father.

Response: *Amen*[17]

---

16 *Maitiro Okuviga Munhu*, p. 31.
17 *Ibid.*, pp. 32-33.

This prayer is followed by other prayers. I will refer to the most important one, which is called the *Mherekedzo* (prayer of accompaniment).

3. Prayer of Accompaniment

Leader: *Lord have mercy*
Response: *Lord have mercy*
Leader: *Christ have mercy*
Response: *Christ have mercy*
Leader: *Lord have mercy*
Response: *Lord have mercy*
Leader: *Grant him/her eternal peace Lord*
Response: *May the Holy light shine upon him/her for ever more*
Leader: *May he/she rest in peace*
Response: *Amen*
Leader: *Holy Mary, here is your child x.*
Response: *Accompany him/her to God.*
Leader: *You his fathers who died recently and all his ancestors on his/her father's lineage here is your child.*
Response: *Accompany him/her to God.*
Leader: *To all his/her maternal ancestors, here is your child.*
Response: *Accompany him/her to God.*
Leader: *All you x's relatives and friends who are dead, here is your relative.*
Response: *Accompany him/her to God.*[18]

This prayer goes on to invoke the personal saint of the deceased and the angels and saints to accompany the deceased to God and to intercede on his/her behalf. The prayer concludes with a petition to Christ.

Leader:

Our Lord Jesus Christ, you taught us saying, "Ask you shall be given, knock it shall be opened". We ask your Father, the God of Heavens, our creator, to forgive x all his/her sins, and that you open the door unto heaven, so that he/she can enter and join in the joys of the angels and

---

[18] *Ibid.*, pp. 33-4.

saints and all his relatives who departed before him/her. Please convey our petition to God the Father.

Response: *Amen.*[19]

This prayer is followed by singing and praying the litany of saints. As the mourners approach the graveyard, the leader instructs the pall-bearers to place the coffin by the grave. He/She then leads the mourners in a prayer for the protection of the grave from desecration.

4. Prayer of protection of the grave

The leader may read a relevant passage from the scriptures and preach by the graveside. He/she then leads the mourners in a prayer to God asking for the protection of the grave in which the body is going to be interred.

Leader:

Let us pray. Lord Jesus Christ, you taught us that you are the life and the resurrection, and that you are the way to the Father. We present to you our relative x for whom you died on the cross. He/she has been called by you Father. Lead him/her to paradise where he/she will live forever more. Lead him/her out of this world of death into the world of eternal life. Your blood was shed on the cross; let it wash away his/her sins. May the cross that you carried for him/her lighten his/her judgement. We pray that he/she be spared the fires of hell and all the judgements that follow after death. Let him/her derive the joys of heaven that you promised all those who have received baptism in water and the Holy spirit.

Response: *Amen.*[20]

This prayer is followed by the blessing of the grave.

5. Blessing the grave

(a) Leader: *Glory be to God*

Response: *Forever and ever.*

Leader: *Let us pray.*

Lord God, the creator of Heaven and earth. This is the house of rest for your child x where we are laying him/her. May your angels protect it from

19 ZCBC, Minamato, Gweru: Mambo Press, 1987, p. 257.

20 *Maitiro Okuviga Munhu*, pp. 39-40.

his/her enemies. In the name of the Father, and of the Son and the Holy Spirit.

Response: *Amen.*[21]

The leader then sprinkles Holy water into the grave saying;

(b) Leader:

I sprinkle this "home" with holy water so that it is sanctified by God. In the name of the Father, and of the Son and of the Holy Spirit.

Response: *Amen.*[22]

If a cross is available, the priest/leader blesses it saying

c) Leader:

This cross is a sign of your deliverance through Christ, and of the hope in your resurrection on the day of the resurrection of all the saints. In the name of the Father, and of the Son and of the Holy spirit.

Response: *Amen.*[23]

The final stage involves the burial of the deceased. At this stage the leader instructs the pall-bearers to lower the coffin into the grave. He/she then accompanies the action by a prayer.

6. *Burial prayers*

(a) Leader: (addressing the deceased)

Enter into your house, and rest in peace until you are raised by Christ on the day of the resurrection of all saints.[24]

The mourners then sing burial songs after which the leader once again leads mourners in prayer.

(b) Leader:

Let us pray. Lord, we have accompanied our relative and we leave him/her with you. He/she is yours. We have finished what we had to do. Lord, pro-

---

21 *Ibid.*, p. 40.
22 *Ibid.*
23 *Ibid.*
24 *Ibid.*

tect all his children, nephews and nieces, and all his/her relatives and friends, as well as his enemies and all of us who are here today?[25]

The leader shifts attention to the deceased and in a direct invocation asks him/her to act as guardian of the family he/she leaves behind.

(c) Leader:

You x pray to God for the protection of the family that you have left here on earth. Pray always that this family be defended from all misfortunes of this world and from all things that harm the spirit and the body. Welcome them on the day of their death and lead them to heaven where there is eternal happiness.

Response: *Amen.*[26]

The leader then throws a handful of soil into the grave. Family members join in, followed by all other relatives and friends. This act symbolizes that burial is a community affair and not just for a few individuals. When this is over, the in-laws and other friends fill up the grave. Other mourners sing before going back to the homestead. This marks the end of the burial rite.

The Christological Character of the Burial Rite

It is clear that the burial rite in its inculturated form was formulated along the perceived roles attributed to ancestors within Shona religion. Prayer 1 and 3 patently manifest this deep-seated belief in the ancestors. However, a closer look at these prayers will show that the ancestral role has been transformed. The ancestors referred to in prayer 1 are only those who are "in God's presence", not all the ancestors of the family of the deceased.

Those ancestors who are in God's presence are deemed worthy of veneration by the family of the deceased and the whole congregation see it fit, therefore, to appeal to them for the assistance and guidance of the deceased on his/her journey to God. Death is therefore viewed as a liminal stage at which the family and the congregation can only play a role of commendation while the ancestors play the role of welcoming the deceased into God's kingdom.

---

25 *Ibid.*
26 *Ibid.*

The problem with this prayer, however, is that it does not make any reference to Christ. The picture painted by the silence regarding Christ can only be that the ancestors in God's presence are given too much power to the extent that they take over Christ's functions as the gateway to God (cf. Jn 10:9) To attribute to the ancestors the duty to receive the deceased into the kingdom of God, within a Christian framework, seems to me to be a downright over-rating of their status.

Related to the problem raised above, is the belief that the deceased himself/herself has the capacity to "shield others from the misfortunes of the world" apart from interceding with God on their behalf. Such faith in the power of the dead further adumbrates the role and status of Christ in the deliverance and welfare of the bereaved.

Prayer 3 begins with a call upon Mary to accompany the deceased to God. In modern Roman Catholic devotion, Mary is considered to be the mediatress of all grace and the channel through which Catholics send their prayers to heaven. Hence the prayer, "Holy Mary, Mother of God, pray for us sinners now and at the hour of our death. Amen."[27]

In Catholic popular piety angels and saints also function as "intermediaries and go-betweens", pleading the petitioners' case before God.[28] In view of the fact that guardian angels and saints are believed to be good spirits, it is not surprising to note that ancestors (those that are with God) are also called upon in this prayer to accompany the deceased to God. The paternal as well as maternal ancestors of the deceased are, therefore, effectively incorporated within the traditional Catholic cult of the saints.

The Catholic belief that God is reflected in His creatures and that grace abounds everywhere is likely to have necessitated the inclusion of ancestors (those "holy souls" with God) within the ranks of angels and saints. The belief in "holy souls" as "revealing spirits" is in itself part of the traditional Catholic sense of "organic community which believes in a network of intimate relationships, not only with those who share the world with us but also with those who have gone before us".[29]

The "holy souls" included in the first part of prayer 3, (i.e. Holy Mary, the personal saint and the guardian angel, other saints and angels, paternal

---

27 J. Pelikan, *The Riddle of Roman Catholicism*, New York: Abingdon, 1959, p. 138.

28 A. Greeley and N. Durkin-Greeley, *How to Save the Catholic Church*, New York: Viking Penguin, 1984, p. 242.

29 *Ibid.*, pp. 232f.

and maternal ancestors, and finally relatives and friends who are with God) are entitled to the veneration of the Church. They are not, however, objects of worship, for worship is only for God (Lat. *latria*) It seems proper therefore for the prayer to shift the attention of the mourners, in its second part, from the "holy souls" to "the Lord of Heaven, our creator" who, through Christ, can forgive x's sins and open the door to Heaven.

Although prayer 3 can be considered as having a sound Christological grounding, there is a problem in the order of intercessors. Within Shona culture, ancestors are invoked beginning with the most junior and ending up with the most senior, who if necessary, convey the message/s to *Mwari* (the Shona High God). Prayer 3, however, begins with Holy Mary and ends with, apparently, the most junior mediators. A properly inculturated prayer would have to be in tune with the Shona world-view and, therefore, the hierarchy of mediators should begin from bottom to the top, not vice-versa.

Unlike prayer 1 which merely makes glib references to "God's kingdom", and also talks of, "the joys and happiness of the righteous", prayer 3 ranks Christ at the apex of the chain of mediators to God the Father. In this prayer, Christ has effectively been made, not merely an ancestor, but the Supreme ancestor who is closest to God.

Prayer 2 begins with an affirmation of the trinitarian nature of the Christian God. It further calls upon God the Father to exercise mercy upon the deceased. That petition is, however, conveyed directly through Christ, the Supreme ancestor.

Prayer 4 carries a more forthright Christological character which portrays Christ as "the life and resurrection" and "the way to the Father". Christ is also portrayed as the liberator who 'leads' the deceased out of the world of mortality to eternal life. One also gets a sense that Christ is the ultimate Victor (*Christus Victor*) since he is referred to as the only one who can save the deceased from the fires of hell and the only one capable of cleansing the deceased of his/her sins.

Prayers 5 and 6 sequence beautifully, leading to the Christian hope in the resurrection of the saints. However, prayer 5(a) appears to be a feeble answer to the fears that the Shona people have regarding the desecration of the grave where their relative lies. Desecration is believed to occur through acts of witches. These are the "enemies" from whom the grave has to be protected. Naturally ancestors, as benign spirits, are attributed the power to protect the grave and the body from "enemies". What seems to be missing in prayer 5(a) is the role of the ancestors, the deceased's personal saint and guardian angel and Holy Mary in the protection of the grave and the body, under the banner of Christ. The reference to angels as protectors is apparently out of tandem with the aspirations of prayer 2.

The last prayer [i.e. 6(a), (b) and (c)] highlights the bereaved's concern with the welfare of the deceased as well as his/her dependants and other family members. However, the order of the prayers appears to be mixed up. If (c) were to replace (b) there would be a better sequence. Subsequently there would be a need to create another prayer which would become (c), the purpose of which would be to appeal to the venerated holy souls (i.e. ancestors, saints and angels and Mary) to protect the family that the deceased used to worship with. In this light, prayer (b) could therefore have become prayer (a).

To have prayer 5(b) become (d), thus constituting the last section in the whole burial rite, is sensible in two ways. Firstly, the words, "we have finished what we had to do" should be seen to be marking the end of the family and the Church's obligations to bury their dead relative and friend. Secondly, the prayer concludes the burial rite in a way that clearly affirms the lordship of Christ over the welfare of the deceased and his/her family and former fellow worshippers.

Conclusion

The burial rite discussed above illustrates the complexity of the process of inculturation, especially in cases where the Christian gospel encounters an ancestor-based worldview like that of the Shona. What the efforts of the Catholic Church in Zimbabwe and the criticisms of this author cumulatively illustrate, is the recognition that inculturation can never be a once-and-for-all event. To be authentic, the Christian gospel has to consistently interrogate, engage and reflect on the worldview that it encounters. The burial rite discussed above is in constant need of adjustment so that this very innovative effort can be furnished with a sounder Christological grounding consistent with the demands of Christian orthodoxy.

Shadipinge Teaches Theology: Biblical Exegesis from an African Cultural Perspective

Obed Kealotswe

Introduction

The search for an Indigenous African Theology has been going on now for some time. The focus, however, has been on African Traditional Religion (ATR) and its relation to Christianity. Most of the works of John Mbiti[1] and Setiloane[2] have tried to show the significance or the importance of ATR to Christianity. These works were prompted by the fact that to many Western theologians and especially missionaries, the Africans had no concept of God and only needed to be taught the Western beliefs and practices. These works have tried to prove beyond any doubt that the Africans had a clear knowledge of God. The important thing that is still missing in African Theology is doctrinal development from an African perspective. Very few works have ever directly addressed this problems. Setiloane posed a great question as to when African Theologians will develop doctrines from their own African traditional religious view.[3]

After this appeal, a wonderful work on Christology from an African perspective was done by Charles Nyamiti.[4] This is one of the few and comprehensive works on doctrine from an African perspective. Nyamiti sees Jesus Christ as Ancestor.[5] One may not necessarily agree with him on some issues, but great recognition should be given to this work. The

---

1 John Mbiti, *An Introduction to African Religion*, Nairobi: Heinemann, 1975, pp. 40-43, discusses the nature of God and names according to many African cultures.

2 Gabriel Setiloane, *Images of God among the Sotho-Tswana*, Rotterdam: Balkema, 1975.

3 Setiloane asks, "Where are we in African Theology? .... the future of African Theology lies in digging it out and presenting it to the World", in Kofi Appiah-Kubi and Sergio Torres (eds), *African Theology en Route*, Maryknoll: Orbis, 1979, p. 64.

4 Charles Nyamiti, *Christ as our Ancestor. Christology from an African Perspective*, Gweru: Mambo, 1984.

5 *Ibid.*, Nyamiti says, "the Ancestorship of Christ makes us His brother-descendants also by instilling into us the responsibility of regular sacred communication with Him in His Spirit".

second important work from a doctrinal point of view is by a white scholar. I refer to Aylward Shorter.[6] He deals with the healing Ministry of Jesus Christ and sees him as a traditional healer. Shorter argues that Jesus healed in the manner of his contemporaries.[7] There was no scientific medicine during his time. He used healing methods used by the traditional healers of that time. Two doctrines are addressed here. These are healing and Christology, viewed from an African perspective. One of the few works I wish to mention is that of Kwame Bediako.[8] This book is a classic in the sense that it is the first to view second century Christian thought from a cultural perspective. Bediako sees a strong connection between culture and the development of Christian thought. In this manner, he emphasizes the importance of the African culture to African Christology. These are the few works that I wish to use as a basis for analysing my research experience and findings in Botswana. The Church of Christ, which is at the centre of my story, is a good example to show that African culture can be very resistant to external pressures.

The narrative that follows is not unique to Ngamiland. It is common to the whole country of Botswana. The narrative is a practical example of a direct contact and struggle between African culture and Western Christianity. Shadipinge is found every where in Africa. Shadipinge is the Sembukushu name for the devil. It is also used to denote a traditional healer, *ngaka*. The traditional healer, *ngaka* is identified by the axe-handle *mhinyana*, that he always carries, even in the church, if he is a Christian. The *mhinyana* is not, however, useful without the axe, nor the axe useful without the *mhinyana*. The traditional healer *ngaka*, therefore, carries the axe with its (*mhinyana*) to make it useful. The belief of the Hambukushu is that the devil always carries an axe in order to kill people. He is Shadipinge, the one who carries an axe. The traditional healer *ngaka* is also called Shadipinge because he cherishes old traditions and religious beliefs and practices which are condemned by the Bible as evil.

---

6 Aylward Shorter, *Jesus and the Witchdoctor. An Approach to Healing and Wholeness*, London: Geoffrey Chapman, 1985.

7 In the preface to his book Shorter states: "In a certain sense Jesus was a medicine man but he was far from being just that. He went beyond all forms of healing, scientific, known to offer a new perspective on wholeness itself," (p. #sentence seems to have been badly copied, wrote to Kealo 5.4.98)

8 Kwame Bediako, *Theology and Identity. The Impact of Culture upon Christian Thought in the Second Century and in Modern Africa*, Oxford: Regnum, 1992.

This paper demonstrates both the negative and positive elements of Biblical exegesis. The paper is based on a study done in Shakawe on the teachings of the Church of Christ, *Phuthego ya ga Keresete*, on its doctrine of baptism and its relationship to faith and Christian living. The doctrine of baptism as elaborated by the use of the example of Shadipinge here, refers to traditional healer and not the devil, as the original meaning denotes. Let us now examine how this doctrine is developed in the Biblical exegesis of the *Phuthego ya ga Keresete*.

Baptism

Key passages: (Jn 3:5; Mk 16:16; Acts 2:38; Mt 28:19-20 and Rom 6:3-4). John 3:5 reads thus:

> Jesus answered, "Truly, truly, I say to you, unless one is born of water and the spirit, he can not enter the kingdom of God".

The understanding of this passage, by the Church of Christ, is that one has first of all to be baptized. Baptism is *mhinyana* (axe-handle). In addition to baptism, there must be the spirit which is the axe itself. Baptism alone, without the spirit, is useless. The spirit gives the gift of speaking in tongues, but it also gives faith in Jesus Christ as the only saviour. Baptism alone, which is regarded by the Church of Christ as the washing away of sins, is useless because it is only *mhinyana* (axe-handle) without an axe. For a Christian to be useful, there must be both baptism and the Holy Spirit which brings faith.

The problem addressed by this paper arises from the argument and observation of the Church of Christ that contrary to the beliefs of the Church that Baptism and the Holy Spirit are the signs of the assurance of salvation, the Hambukushu *ngaka* or Shadipinge, still carries his traditional axe, even after baptism. The expectation of the church is that after baptism, all the traditional values and beliefs should give way to the new life in Jesus Christ. Is this the same way in which the Hambukushu understand or conceive salvation?

Before addressing the question above, let us examine one other passage used by the Church of Christ. This is Mark 16:16-18. The passage states that those who believe and are baptized, will be saved, while those who do not believe, will be condemned. The passage also states the signs of salvation which include the casting out of demons, speaking in tongues, picking up serpents without being hurt, drinking deadly poison without being hurt and laying hands on the sick and they are healed.

To go back to the question asked above, the Hambukushu, like other Africans, believe in the existence of God who is the creator and originator of all things. This God lives above in the heavens. The approach to this God is through the ancestors, *badimo*, who communicate with the people through the *ngaka* or Shadipinge. The Church of Christ, preaches Jesus Christ as the Saviour and only mediator before God for all the believers. Shadipinge accepts this teaching because it does not deny the existence of God who is revealed via human beings like Jesus Christ who lived on earth and then ascended to heaven. Shadipinge, like Nyamiti,[9] understands Jesus Christ as the great ancestor. There is nothing wrong in convincing Shadipinge that the ancestors are lower than Jesus Christ in the hierarchy. If the ancestors are lower than Jesus Christ, they still remain in the hierarchy and Shadipinge sees them as closing the gap between him and Jesus Christ in the hierarchy. Shadipinge feels that he cannot approach Jesus Christ, directly but through the ancestors, since Jesus is also equated with God who cannot be approached directly. The ancestors, therefore, still remain in the hierarchy and there is nothing wrong in honouring them by the axe because they are also under Jesus. The Church of Christ does not teach that all the ancestors are condemned and they are in hell because they were not baptized. In actual fact, I have never heard of a church which preaches this doctrine. This lack of a clear stand on the fate of the ancestors is a problem that has led not only African Christianity, but also Western Christianity, to continue to honour the ancestors. In Western culture, Paul's teaching that those who lived before Christ will be judged by their conscience, is believed in Western Christianity. This is also echoed by the great apologist Justin Martyr who claims that even the Greek philosophers had some knowledge of God which they learned from the Hebrew prophets.[10] The same belief is shared by Philo of Alexandria.[11] This uncertainty about the fate of the ancestors is more of a problem with African Christianity whose world-view is not far from that of Biblical times. Jesus, in his teaching on the kingdom of God, states that the king-

---

9 Nyamiti, *Christ as our Ancestor*, p. 25.

10 J. Gonzalez, *A History of Christian Thought*, Vol. 1, Nashville: Abingdon, pp. 104-106.

11 *Ibid.*, pp. 43f.

dom is present and at the same time as eschatological. By so saying, he recognizes continuity in life which agrees very well with the African world-view. The belief in the ancestors and their continued existence, also agrees with Paul that the dead are asleep and they will be the ones to come with Christ when he comes for the second time to judge the living and the dead (1 Thess. 4:15-17).

Such teaching is not strange to Shadipinge who recognizes the existence of the ancestors as mediators between him and Jesus Christ. The early church actually regarded itself as the chosen race in the Judaic sense. Jesus himself claimed that he had not come to abolish the law, but to fulfil it. This is a law which was given by the Old Testament God who according to Marcion,[12] was a jealous and cruel God who taught revenge and the sacrifice of children. This same God has revealed himself in Jesus Christ and Jesus Christ traces his linkage to all the Hebrew ancestors. These Hebrew ancestors, as read by Shadipinge from the Old Testament, had beliefs and practices similar to his. They had rules regarding the birth of babies, rules regarding a woman under confinement and how that woman (Lev. 12:1-8) and the baby had to be reinstated into the society. The Old Testament teaches how to approach God or Yahweh with different sacrifices meant to please Yahweh the Lord. Respect for the tombs of the ancestors is also recognized by the Old Testament. Above all, the priests of the Old Testament have special garments which they must wear and they also carry staffs as prescribed by Yahweh. Shadipinge carries his axe as a symbol of his special role which he plays in the society. Going to church does not make him relinquish his practices and beliefs which are only expressed in a new form by Christianity. In all respects there is nothing new and surprising to Shadipinge. The problem with the Church of Christ and some AICs is that Shadipinge is looked at negatively, yet the Old Testament is not disregarded but always seen as a prelude to the New Testament. The practices of the Hebrews in the Old Testament are not labelled as devilish but they are seen as leading to Jesus Christ. But the African beliefs and practices, which are in many respects similar to those of the Old Testament, are labelled as devilish. Shadipinge does not agree with this but sees Christ as the embodiment of his ancestors.

---

12 *Ibid.*, p. 141.

The other interesting belief of Shadipinge concerns the above summary of Mark 16:16-18. Speaking in tongues is not anything new to Shadipinge because he divines the ancestors to give him the power to speak in tongues. The main duty of Shadipinge is to heal the sick. Shadipinge also performs miracles and magic. He can create serpents or make serpents harmless, he can give medicine to people that even if they drank poison, they would not die. All these are gifts that come to Shadipinge from God, through Jesus and the ancestors. In this manner, Shadipinge feels very comfortable in the Church of Christ. One other thing is that the gift of the Holy Spirit is expressed by possession which makes people dance, jump around and shout etc. This behaviour is not strange to Shadipinge because he also sings, dances and shouts when possessed by the Holy Spirit from the ancestors. In this manner he feels very comfortable in the Church of Christ.

Romans 6:3-4 talks about baptism in Jesus Christ, bringing a newness of life. Ritual washing is a process which Shadipinge has gone through during his initiation. Baptism to him is also a ritual which brings the newness in life where Jesus becomes greater than the ancestors. This, however, to Shadipinge does not minimize the role and respect to the ancestors. Instead, their role is strengthened because they become part of the hierarchy. Jesus, as well as the ancestors, are all recognized by Shadipinge as his mediators before God. In this manner Shadipinge finds no contradictions between his own traditional religious beliefs and those of Christianity as preached and practised by the Church of Christ. The Church of Christ, however, does not recognize this inculturation of the Gospel message. Instead, Shadipinge is criticized for carrying his axe after baptism and having gained membership of the church. Shadipinge is seen as a bad person who still sticks to the old, while the Church of Christ is adopting the American ways of belief and practice. My informants always depicted Western beliefs as Christianity. This belief, by the Church of Christ that African culture is bad and Christianity is only compatible with Western culture, makes the Church face a lot of problems with the Hambukushu because they understand Christianity from their own cultural perspective. This is helped by the fact that the Hebrew culture as shown in the Old Testament, is compatible with Hambukushu culture. In African Christianity, especially in the AICs, the Old Testament is central because it is a fulfilment and consolation of African and, especially, Hambukushu culture. The New Testament is understood and interpreted in its relation to the Old

Testament. To the Hambukushu and especially to Shadipinge, the New Testament has meaning only if it is interpreted and related to the Old Testament. Relating the New Testament to the Old Testament also relates the Gospel message to African culture. Some churches, like the Roman Catholic Church in Gaborone, have accepted the fact that Shadipinge can still be a good Catholic as well as practising in accordance with his understanding of the place of the ancestors within the Christian hierarchy.[13]

In conclusion, there is a felt need among many African Theologians that Christianity must become an African Religion, lived and understood or conceived within African heritage. To a great extent, the theology of the AICs has made this wish possible. The only problem is that Western trained African Theologians have a wish which they do not want to see materialize. In my own situation, I enjoy myself when I visit AICs and learn from them. I enjoy myself when I visit Shadipinge for he tells me about all his beliefs and practices. I do appreciate them but do not want to practice them because my mind has been so pumped with Western ideas and concepts that I feel inferior if I also believe and practise the life of the AICs or Shadipinge. This is the struggle that is now facing the African Theologian, i.e. how to disentangle him/herself from the chains of cultural slavery? The survival of the Western theologian lies in Africa and the Third World as a whole. The above is a synopsis of that Theology as cooked by Shadipinge from his own African pot. What are the major lessons from this experience? My observations are:

1. Ordinary African peoples, with little education and exposure to Western culture and values, are the real people from whom an African hermeneutics should emerge. These are people who read the Bible from an African cultural perspective.

2. The impact of the AICs Biblical Exegesis has influenced Botswana Christianity and Tswana has become a good pot for cooking our Theology. This is made possible by great ecumenism experienced among Tswana churches.

---

13 Obed Kealotswe & Byaruhanga-Akiiki, *Healers and Protective Medicine in Botswana*, Department of Theology and Religious Studies, University of Botswana, Gaborone, 1995.

3. African Theologians in the Southern African region have to collect similar exegeses, and live an African Christianity, instead of being second hand Christians of the so-called first world.

In conclusion, let me say that the story of Shadipinge and the Church of Christ in Shakawe is an example of events that are happening in all the areas of our region. This case study challenges us to take Shadipinge seriously and change our theological outlook.

Health and Healing: New Developments in Spirit Mediumship in Malawi

Joseph C. Chakanza

There is misconception and distrust concerning traditional ways of healing in Malawi. The very idea of possession by a spirit, ancestral or otherwise, provokes scepticism. The swing from possession by ancestral spirits to possession by spirits of saints and Biblical personalities among the spirit mediums has made a great impact.

Although it has not yet been positively endorsed by some sections of our community as an alternative system of medical practice contributing to health care, traditional healing is still sought after by many people. Traditional healers claim success in treating such diseases as cancer, diabetes, insanity, asthma, epilepsy, sexually transmitted diseases, conditions of impotence in males and of infertility in females. Official government policy has been to encourage traditional healers to improve and update their healing techniques.[1]

Spirit Mediumship

A recent innovation in traditional healing in Malawi has been detected among some of the spirit mediums (*asing'anga a mizimu*) who have incorporated some Christian elements in their healing ministry.[2] It is this category of spirit mediums that I discuss in this article. The conventional spirit mediums are healers who deal with ancestral spirits and carry out their work of mediumship only when possessed by the spirits. Otherwise, they are normal people. Possession constitutes an important means of communication with the spirit world, a world of invisible beings which can influ-

1 Traditional healers in Malawi have formed the "Herbalists' Association in Malawi" with its sister wing, the "Traditional Birth Attendants". The ministry of Health has appointed a doctor who liaises with them.

2 J.C. Chakanza, "Health and Healing: Spirit Mediumship", *The Lamp*, no. 7, January-March 1997, 24f.

ence people either for good or for evil. Spirit possession, then, is a cultural term which gives expression to the belief that a person who displays certain behaviour has been taken possession of by an invisible being or power.[3] In Malawi, spirit possession which is understood literally as *kugwidwa* or *kulowedwa ndi azimu* is known by different names among various ethnic groups such as *malombo* (Mang'anja, Sena), *mabzyoka*, *chikwangwali*, *mazinda* (Sena), *mpwesa*, *mtume*, *nantongwe* (Lomwe), *majini mutu waukulu* (Yao, Nyanja), *vimbuza*, *virombo*, *nyanusi* (Tumbuka-Ngoni).[4] Although spirit possession is regarded as *matenda* (illness), it may be useful to distinguish between possession cases requiring the permanent expulsion of an undesirable spirit through exorcism and those which aim at establishing some sort of lasting relationship through accomodation. This will separate the phenomenon of spirit mediumship from that of spirit possession in general. In the latter cases the behaviour of the individual concerned does not necessarily convey any particular message to other people. It is primarily regarded as the bodily expression of spirit possession by the possessed person, whereas in the case of the former, the emphasis is on the communicative aspect.[5]

The Call to the Healing Ministry

There is no doubt that changes in our society have had an impact on traditional ways of healing which have adjusted to new circumstances and influences. To illustrate this point, I shall confine myself to the influences of the Christian religion on spirit mediums. The point I want to emphasize briefly is that there has emerged a number of spirit mediums who claim to heal not by being possessed by ancestral spirits, but by personalities mentioned in

---

3 Maureen Wilkinson, *A Mental Health Handbook for Malawi*, Limbe: Assemblies of God Literature Centre Press, 1991, p. 231.

4 On spirit possession among the Sena and Mang'anja, see: J.M. Schoffeleers, "Evil Spirits and Rites of Exorcism in the Lower Shire Valley", mimeo, 1968; Among the Lomwe, see, Athony J. Nazombe, "Nantongwe: a Lomwe Spirit Possession Ritual", *Religion in Malawi*, no. 2, 1988, pp. 15-18; among the Tumbuka - Ngoni, J.B. Soko, "An Introduction to the Vimbuza Phenomenon", *Religion in Malawi*, no. 1, 1987, pp. 9-12; J.B. Soko, "The Vimbuza Possession Cult: The Onset of the Disease", *Religion in Malawi*, no. 2, 1988, pp. 11-15.

5 For a brief discussion on spirit possession, see, G. ter Haar, A. Moyo, S.J. Nondo, *African Traditional Religions in Religious Education. A resource book with special reference to Zimbabwe*, Utrecht University, 1992, pp. 117-127.

the Bible as well as by Christian saints, thereby giving their healing ministry a Christian flavour. Usually they are church-going members and their healing techniques entail the use of prayers, Bible readings, hymn-singing and other Christian practices together with some traditional elements. They are not to be confused with faith healers or ordinary herbalists and neither are they to be considered prophets or founders of new churches. Like the traditional spirit mediums, they did not choose to become healers, but, at a crucial point in their lives, they found that the had no alternative but to accept the 'call' to the healing ministry. Usually, a critical and protracted illness which did not respond to any cure was recognised as a sign of the 'call'. Once it was accepted, the illness ceased, but when this sign was neglected or refused, the illness worsened. In the traditional setting, the 'call' comes from an ancestral spirit while in this new manifestation, it originates from the spirits of saints and persons mentioned in the Bible such as Mary, Lazarus, John the Baptist, James, Thomas, Noah, Melchizedek etc.

Recent research carried out by Bernadette Banda,[6] a Bachelor of Arts student at Chancellor College, on two such spirit mediums at Namitete in Mchinji district, illustrates what I have been saying about this 'call'. The first one, a man whose name is Potifala is a member of the CCAP. He had been critically ill for years and all efforts to cure him through western and traditional medicines were to no avail. In early 1979, he became possessed and the possessing spirit spoke through him saying: "I am the spirit of Lazarus and have come to stay permanently. I want Potifala to become a healer". At first he ignored the 'call' and thereafter his illness became even worse. Later, he became unconscious and the spirit reiterated its demand. He felt he had no choice but to yield. He was then twenty-five years old. He came to be known as 'Lazarus' after the spirit.

The second case-study is that of a Roman Catholic lady, Alfonsina, who became seriously ill in 1987 and was brought to a certain spirit medium called Maria. During one of the sessions for exorcism, as people said prayers, she became possessed and a spirit spoke through her saying "I am the spirit of John and have come to stay permanently. I want Alfonsina to take up witch-identification and witch-chasing as her career."

---

6 Bernadette Banda, "Two Healing Spirit Mediums in Nkhwazi Village: An Assessment of their Ministry", B.A.(Theol), University of Malawi, 1996.

Six weeks later, when Alfonsina had shown reluctance to accept the 'call', she became seriously ill once again. She was brought to Potifala and while prayers for exorcism were being said, she became unconscious. She became possessed and the possessing spirit spoke through her saying: "I am the spirit of John and have come to stay permanently . I want Alfonsina to take up healing as her career." Alfonsina responded to the call and she is functioning as a spirit medium until today.

In Bvumbwe (Thyolo district), the foundress and proprietor of St Maria's Clinic (Chipatala cha Maria) which opened its doors to patients on 9 July, 1984, has a similar story to tell. The spirit of Maria entered her when she become unconscious after undergoing an operation. While she was in that state, the spirit revealed to her many types of medicines for curing a host of diseases. The spirit continues to reveal medicinal herbs to her through dreams. She and her husband are Catholics.[7]

A Healing Session

Unlike the ordinary herbalists who rely on their knowledge of medicinal herbs, spirit mediums rely on dreams and possession to decide on diagnosis and treatment. They have a special room for diagnosis and treatment which is known as *kachisi* (spirit house). When they carry out a healing session, they wear special uniforms: white robes and hats with red crosses marked on them. The *kachisi* has hardly any furniture and patients sit on mats. There are religious symbols such as crosses, pictures of saints, hymn books and copies of the Bible. Shoes and metal objects such as coins are usually not allowed into the *kachisi*. Their presence hinders the healing sessions.

The healing session proper starts with hymn-singing, both traditional and Christian, is meant to invoke the healer spirit to descend with its power and give guidance in the diagnosis and dosage. Spontaneous prayers are made by both patients and attendants. The spirit medium asks one person to read selected texts from the Bible, usually those suited to the occasion. In the course of the Bible reading the spirit medium becomes really possessed and the diagnosis of the patient starts. The patients do not have to tell the spirit medium what their ailments are but wait for him to establish the ver-

7 Lucy Mulanje, "Maria, the Healer at Bvumbwe in Thyolo District", B.Ed., University of Malawi, 1990.

dict. They may disagree with the verdict but when it corresponds with their feelings, they gain confidence in the spirit medium's use mirrors as a sort of video screen where past and present experiences of the patient and other suspicious circumstances can be seen. A stick is also used by some spirit mediums. It is believed that the power of the spirit is transmitted through the stick to help the spirit medium to diagnose properly and administer appropriate medicines. Some spirit mediums wear belts around their waist in the belief that his will lessen pain in the patient being diagnosed.

Conclusion

There is no doubt that these spirit mediums create a Christian atmosphere in the way they exercise their healing ministry. A prayer is said before the actual diagnosis starts; the gathered community is made to sing church hymns; Bible passages are read and heard by Christians and non-Christians alike. However, it is difficult to know what to say concerning the claims of the spirit mediums that the are possessed not by ancestral spirits, but by spirits of saints and personalities found in the Bible. Is this genuine, and can we believe that saints are really at work among these people? The response from mainstream churches has simply been to reject or ignore them and, in many cases, to forbid their followers to approach these mediums while they themselves are ostracized from their churches. However, these spirit mediums are trying to blend Christian and traditional concepts of healing by using symbols from both. Above all, they are suggesting that traditional ways of healing can be changed and improved by contact with other forces, be they positive or negative towards them. There is misconception and distruct concerning traditional ways of healing, presumably because they lack a rationally formulated expression when compared with western medical practice. The very idea of possession by a spirit, ancestral or otherwise, immediately provokes scepticism in many western-oriented people.

Finally, I wish to observe that the spirit mediums do not claim to cure every disease, hence they refer some cases to hospitals. This swing from possession by ancestral spirits to possession by spirits of saints and Biblical personalities among the spirit mediums has made a great impact. It replaces witchcraft and sorcery as well as evil spirits. It helps to build a sound community under Christian influence directly or indirectly by not antagonizing people.

What's in a Name? Naming Practices among African Christians in Zimbabwe

Ezra Chitambo[1]

1. Introduction

The interaction between Christianity and African traditional culture has been the subject of much scholarly discourse. The complex nature of the relationship has given rise to diverse interpretations. While it is generally accepted that Christianity started gaining a stronghold in the Southern African context in the late nineteenth century, controversy surrounds the role of the early missionaries in the implantation of the religion. On the one hand, some scholars accuse the missionaries of cultural prejudice. They argue that most early missionaries regarded African culture as pagan and backward.[2] The only way they perceived of ensuring the success of an unadulterated faith was to dismantle the prevailing culture. On the other hand, there are other scholars who argue that this position is too simplistic - a number of missionaries were pioneers in 'inculturation', 'indigenisation', etc.[3] In an effort to contribute to the on-going debate, this article endeavours to analyse the impact of Christianity in an African culture by isolating one feature, viz. naming practices among black Christians in Zimbabwe. This necessitates a brief historical excursion into the relationship between those who brought the gospel and the local culture.

2. Missionaries and African Culture in General

In order for us to appreciate the dynamism surrounding the quest for identity epitomised by the giving of African names by black Christians in

1 Ezra Chitando is a PhD candidate with the University of Zimbabwe.

2 See, for example, Aylward Shorter, *African Culture and the Christian Church*, Maryknoll: Orbis, 1974, p. 66.

3 See, for example, S. Kaplan, "The Africanisation of Missionary Christianity; History and Typology", *Journal of Religion in Africa*, vol. 16, no. 3, October 1986 and Lamin Sanneh, *Translating the Message*, Maryknoll: Orbis, 1989.

Zimbabwe today, we need to have a brief overview of how missionaries viewed African culture in general. It is difficult to bring out the trend regarding the early missionaries since they were individuals, hence they tended to have different perceptions regarding the indigenous people.

In the area under investigation, i.e., Masvingo in the southern part of Zimbabwe, the Dutch Reformed Church was the first in the area. Morgenster Mission, also known as Mugabe, after the name of the chief, was established in 1891 under the leadership of A.A. Louw.[4] For a long time, the Dutch Reformed Church was the only denomination which held sway in the area. This was in line with the early missionaries' tacit arrangement of not jostling for souls in the same field. From an examination of the missionaries' attitude towards the local culture, it becomes clear that denominational affiliations made little difference. It is also true that the missionaries and the colonial administrators tended to converge in opinion on the disparagement of the indigenous culture. Both were victims of (unintended) absolutisation of their Western culture. Oblivious of the relativism of their own culture, they regarded it as normative. Traditional practices such as name-giving, marriage, dances and so on were all condemned as forms of paganism. Indeed for one to be a Christian one had to sever all ties with traditional culture. According to A. Channels: "To the early missionaries in the century, the adoption of European life styles by the heathen was regarded as one of the fruits of conversion to Christianity."[5] In this initial phase of missionary activity then, Europeanization and conversion were largely coterminous.

Given their low estimation of traditional culture, it is not surprising that the early phase of the missionaries' efforts ended in failure. Among the Karanga, traditional religion was vibrant. The Mwari cult,[6] with its influence over rain in an agriculturally based economy, was a formidable foe. Special sacred practitioners called *manyusa* had control over the crucial resource i.e. rain. In addition, most, if not all Africans, also upheld the honour of the ancestors. The missionaries' emphasis on sin, conversion and

4 D.N. Beach, "The Initial Impact of Christianity on the Shona: The Protestants and the Southern Shona", in J.A. Dachs (ed), *Christianity South of the Zambezi*, Volume 1, Gweru: Mambo, 1973, p. 33.

5 A. Chennells, "The Image of the Ndebele and the Nineteenth Century Missionary Tradition", in M.F.C. Bourdillon (ed.), *Christianity South of the Zambezi*, Vol. 2; Gweru: Mambo, 1977, p. 43.

6 See, for example M.L. Daneel, *God of the Matopos*, Gweru: Mambo, 1977, p. 43.

a new life-style proved remote and unconvincing. What Carnegie, an early missionary, observed of the Ndebele could as well apply to the Karanga,

> The Matabele as a tribe are, practically speaking, in the same position, intellectually and morally, and in every other way, only a little more conceited, than they were thirty years ago.[7]

That the early missionary drive, characterized as it was by education and health, met with such fate, makes a mockery of the popular notion that traditional religions are largely 'ecumenical' and therefore tolerant. Indeed, it was only with the suppression of the Ndebele and Shona uprisings at the turn of the century and the subsequent coming to terms with the reality of western civilisation that, Christianity started making an impact. It may be said, therefore, that whilst some missionaries might have been sympathetic to aspects of African culture, on the whole they were dismissive. They regarded their task as bringing the light of the gospel to a people who were culturally backward.

Conversion to Christianity, when it finally became a possibility after the African military power had been pounded into submission, meant a radical break with the past. Since the traditional culture stood for paganism, the new converts were encouraged to adopt a new life-style which was in line with their 'saved' status. Education was seen as an instrument which would 'detribalize' the African and make him more amenable to the overtures of the gospel. Most, if not all, Africans whom the missionaries dealt with had culture-bound names. This was one practice which most missionaries felt was a clear testimony of the need for a thorough-going transformation of the local culture. Not only were these names difficult to pronounce, they were laden with the socio-religious concerns of the African people. In order to illustrate the missionary attitude to local culture, it becomes necessary to discuss naming practices in the traditional Zimbabwean societies.

3. Naming Practices in Zimbabwean Traditional Religions

In the traditional Shona context, names were not convenient tags to differentiate one individual from the next. Most names were laden with meaning.

---

7 D. Carnegie cites Chennells, *The Image of the Ndelebe*, p. 67.

A.J. Pongweni argues:

> Death, family contradictions and societal rivalries inspired the Shona creative mind no less than the heroism, celebration and cowardice of the battlefield.[8]

It is clear, therefore, that the Shona people gave their children culture bound-names. These names encapsulated the people's socio-religious concerns and were meaningful in their given context. Whilst generalizations are often dangerous, one may argue that this was the trend amongst other African people. Indeed, even names of places and animals were of special significance. Along the Mutirikwi River there is a spot known as Bikiro (the brewing place) where elders used to brew beer in honour of the ancestors. Names given to cattle and dogs also captured the owner's history, achievements and frustrations. However, the names of the people were the greatest religious carriers. J.S. Mbiti identifies the different circumstances which determined a child's names.[9] His outline is useful and shall be employed to delineate the types of names given to children in the traditional Shona culture. It is therefore necessary to highlight the importance of the arrival of the child.

(a) Arrival and naming of the child

In the traditional Shona society the institution of marriage had clear religious overtones. Children were regarded as a special blessing and infertility was seen as a fundamental human problem which necessitated intervention governed by specific rules of behaviour and the mid-wife (*nyamukuta*) was a specialised sacred practitioner. Before accepting the baby into his world, she was supposed to express her appreciation of the role of the ancestors and to clap her hands as a mark of respect. She would utter a few words, calling upon the baby's ancestors to facilitate a safe delivery. Ululation and clapping signified the arrival of the baby from the ancestral realm. In the traditional Karanga context, a child would only be named after about eight days. Whilst the exact religious explanation is difficult to unravel, it might have had to with a rather high degree of infant mortality. Before this the baby was confined to the hut where the birth had taken

---

8 A.J. Pongweni, *What's in a Name*, Gweru: Mambo, 1983, p. 29.

9 J.S. Mbiti, *Introduction to African Religions*, 2nd ed., Nairobi: East African Educational Publishers, 1992, pp. 92-95.

place. It was with the naming ceremony that the baby was introduced to society and was considered *munthu* (a person) with rights and responsibilities like all other members of society. As noted earlier, the name was never chosen at random. It was chosen with care and usually served to summarise the feelings of the parents, circumstances surrounding birth and various other considerations. We follow Mbiti's categorization of names below:[10]

(b) Names reflecting the feeling of the parents

Most Shona parents gave their children names which reflected their own situation, ideals and frustrations. a child's name could therefore capture the vicissitudes of life. A couple living in a hostile community could name their child Zvamada (whatever you have decided) as a sign that they are prepared for whatever course of action the opponents might take. Musiyiwa (the one left behind) would be given to one orphaned around birth. In the event of a family having an only child, he/she could be named Zindoga (the lonely one). As a reminder to their detractors, a child could be named Tarisai (look at our accomplishments). Indeed, a couple had a litany of names to chose from whenever they wanted to express their feelings. The names could also have clear religious meaning as in Tapiwa (we have been given). Such names captured the dependence of the parents on the ancestors. Other names were in the form of prayers or expressions of gratitude.

(c) Names relating to the time and place of birth

While the Shona people certainly noted a distinction between religious time and profane time, the time of a child's birth was accorded a special place. If it so happened that the mother experienced labour pains and gave birth by the road-side, the child could be called Chenzira (of the road). Mid-day is regarded as sacred time and a child born at this time could be called Masakati (afternoon). A name could also reflect the events prevailing at the time of birth, e.g., the peoples' experience of the Ndebele raids or of the Chimurenga war that led to names such as Hondo (war).

(d) Names that show religious feelings

These closely related to names which reflected the feelings of the parents.

---

10 *Ibid.*

In this category, one comes across religiously charged names. This was particularly true when a couple named a child after a departed ancestor. According to informants, this was when the child had features which reminded people of the deceased. In certain instances, people could actually remark that the child was an incarnation of the deceased, e.g., *Mwana uyu ndiChitsamatoro* accurately describes the honour bestowed upon the child. "Among the Shona, the respect due to such a child, if named after an ancestor, is shown by how all address it by using the honorific plural."[11] Such a child, by virtue of the name, could be called upon to officiate in some rituals since he or she was "an elder". Informants pointed out that people who engaged in socially-unacceptable activities such as witchcraft and sorcery could not expect relatives to name children after them. There were fears that their personalities would be mystically transferred to the child. Indeed, when a child named after a rogue character exhibited similar tendencies, the elders would revoke the name and replace it with another one. A behavioural change in the child was anticipated. Other names mark the habit of the child, for example, a child who cried incessantly might be named Jemedza (one given to crying). Names like Nhamo (poverty) indicated the economic status of the parents. Nicknames were given later in life and described a person's character or inclinations, for example, Gararirimo (one who stays with it inside) referred to one who was perpetually drunk. It can therefore be noted that names in traditional Shona culture were an invaluable reservoir of the people's social and religious experience. While more examples could be cited in support of the statement, it should suffice to add that children were warned never to respond when their name was called at night. It w as believed that witches could mystically use the name to further their nefarious activities and harm the intended victim. How were the early missionaries to react to this deep-rooted and dearly-held practice?

IV. Early Missionaries and Indigenous Names

It would seem that in the early phase of the encounter between the missionaries and the local population, the issue of names was a peripheral one. The missionaries just had one major preoccupation - to preach the gospel. As

---

11 Pongweni, *What's in a Name*, p. 3.

such they were not worried about the names of their potential converts. This was particularly true of the time when most elderly African people distanced themselves from the new faith. At this stage, the task was to try and woo as many converts to the faith as was possible. A glance at the names of some of the earliest converts shows that most kept their indigenous names. This was bound to change when the new faith made significant in-roads. The rite of baptism presented an opportunity for the convert to change his or her name for a "Christian one". During baptism, the convert was reminded that he or she was now a "new creation" and that the old person had died.

A new name, reminiscent of Saul who became known as Paul (Acts 13:9), was seen as an essential indication of the transition from heathenism to a new life. However, most of the names were biblical and western. Most missionaries taught the converts to identify with biblical figures, particularly the apostles. One, therefore, finds that names such as John, James, Peter, Paul and others were common. Among female converts names like Martha, Mary and others occur often. Madziyire narrates the story of medium of the influential Kasosa spirit who said the following words on his death-bed: "I have been baptised and my new name is Abraham."[12] He also has another respondent who makes the following declaration: "My heathen name is Matinetsa Mahere. My Christian name is Grace."[13]

While it is clear that most converts chose the names of biblical characters, a considerable number simply went for (or were given) non-Christian, European names. The tradition within which a particular missionary was stemmed went a very long way in determining his choice of names for the new converts. According to H. Bhila, the initial contact of Christianity and Southern Zambezia only started in the later half of the 16th century through the work of Father Gonçalo da Silveira. The young emperor Negomo Mupunzaguta was converted to Christianity with his mother: "Both he and his mother were baptised after which they assumed the names of Sebasti ⊧o and Luisa respectively."[14] One can, therefore, note that the practice of requiring converts to change names has a long history in Christianity and

---

[12] S.K. Madziyire, "African Religious Practices and Christianity among the Shona People", in J.A. Dachs (ed.), *Christianity South of the Zambezi*, Vol. 1, Gweru: Mambo, 1973, p. 127.

[13] Ibid., p. 131.

[14] H. Bhila, "Trade and the Early Missionaries in Southern Zambezi", in M.F.C. Bourdillon (ed.), *Christianity South of the Zambezi*, Vol. 2, Gweru: Mambo, 1977, p. 25.

cuts across denominations. It would seem most early missionaries were not motivated by the "heathen" nature of culture-bound names as they were by the need to inculcate in the convert a sense of being "born again". Apart from the expressly religious concerns associated with baptism, there were other reasons why more and more African had to forsake their traditional names.

Education and Traditional Names

It has been noted that Christianity started to have a considerable impact after the suppression of the 1896-97 African uprisings. From then on most African elders grudgingly accepted the reality of western influence. Most of them distanced themselves from Christianity, the mission schools and hospitals. However, they encouraged their children to master whatever secrets the *vauyi* (newcomers) had to import. By so doing the area of education benefitted greatly.

The African who enrolled in a mission school faced a plethora of problems. He or she was uprooted from the familiarity of the village into the new world of the western tradition. Most African writers agree that an overwhelming majority of those who had tasted the 'sweetness' of western culture were quick to denounce their culture-bound names in favour of European ones. Traditional Shona names were a source of shame and embarassment for many. Indeed, stories abound of parents who visited their children at school and had difficulties in locating them since they had assumed new names! The "village name" was therefore a closely guarded secret. This practice continues even today. A considerable number of people substitute their old names with English ones. The alternative is to shorten one's Shona name so that it sounds English or simply exotic. While more examples could be cited, the following observation by G. ter Haar should suffice: "Western education undermined African traditional society in many ways and the school played a particular role in that process."[15]

It was the western-educated African parent who in turn gave his or her child a European name as a reflection of this newly-acquired "knowledge". Most black Zimbabweans born in the pre-independence era (before 1980) have English names. However, as noted above, some of the names reflect a

---

[15] Gerrie ter Haar, *The Faith of Our Fathers*, Utrecht: Faculteit der Godgeleerdheid, 1990, p. 40.

Christian orientation. Others, however, are almost tragic. The writer came across a farm labourer who named his first-born son Lavatory. While the name is indicative of the place where the birth took place, it is clear that the father was keen to have any English name for his child. Due to the practice of *Sazita* (name sake), European names have persisted. One can therefore note that through conversion to Christianity and western education, most Africans tended to shun their traditional names. The nationalist struggle sought to arrest this cultural malaise.

V. The Nationalist Struggle and African Names

The colonial enterprise in Africa had always met with some resistance from the indigenous people. That it succeeded was due to the collapse of empires and the superior firepower it had assembled. In Zimbabwe the Ndebele and Shona uprisings of 1896-97 are properly seen as foreshadowing the armed struggle which reached its peak in the late 1970s. That the leaders of the Mwari cult and the spirit mediums Nehanda and Kaguvi were influential in the earlier uprisings, meant that the religious dimension would be present in the latter. When the nationalist cause was gaining momentum in the 1960s, symbols from traditional religions were used to add fervour and zeal. Leaders like Joshua Nkomo and Robert Mugabe used snuff, the walking rod and *ngundu* (royal head-gear) at public meetings. This was to portray themselves as the rightful heirs to the lost throne. At the heart of the dispute was the land issue and land, ideologically, belonged to the ancestors.[16]

Both the nationalist mobilisation and the subsequent liberation struggle were portrayed as a deliberate reclamation of African values which had been trampled upon by the joint forces of Christianity and colonialism. During this phase, some Africans publicly denounced their English names in favour of African ones. Others also attacked Christianity for being part and parcel of the colonial enterprise. However, it must be noted that this change of names was not at a large-scale. This was not because people did not understand that their names were 'loaded'. Most of the nationalist had Christian backgrounds and found their Christian names meaningful. As an

---

16 See, for example, J.M. Schoffeleers (ed.), *Guardians of the Land: Essays on Central African Territorial Cults*, Gweru: Mambo, 1978.

act of deference to parents, most chose to simply uphold their English names. This was in line with the traditional concept we discussed earlier in which a name is very much part of a person's identity.

The combatants on the battle-front, however, changed their names. This was in line with their task of liberating the motherland. Most of them adopted Shona names. According to Pongweni: "The latter differed from the pre-colonial names in that they were names of resistance and protest."[17] Security reasons also necessitated the change of names. These combatants adopted names like Gidi Ndirochete "the gun is the only answer", Teurai Ropa "spill blood", Tamuka Vatema "we the black people have arisen" and many other colourful and meaningful Shona names. This was done alongside a revitalisation of many ancestral practices by the combatants. Heroes of the first resistance were invoked as in the song *Nehanda dzikamudzimu* (Nehanda, establish the ancestral power). Due to the Maoist and Marxist teaching received during training in Mozambique, combatants attacked Christianity as "the white man's religion". However, the Marxist ideal of the obliteration of religion could not be achieved overnight, hence the attempted technique of 'elimination by substitution'. While some work has been done,[18] a full history of the use of traditional religions in Zimbabwe's war of liberation is yet to be written. For the purposes of this presentation, it is important to note the significance of names in African society may be seen during the phase of the armed struggle when combatants took new, culture-bound names. This practice was to be pronounced among African Christians with the attainment of political independence in 1980.

Political Independence and African Christian Names

When one studies any class list of primary school pupils in Zimbabwe today, one is struck by the wealth of information which most names provide. A number of names are recurrent, for example Tatenda (we are greatful), Tafadzwa (we have been made happy), Nyasha (Grace) and Simbarashe (God's power). Most pupils have Shona names. In addition, most of the names are charged with Christian concepts. It is significant to

---

17 Pongweni, *What's in a Name*, p. 2.

18 See, for example, D. Lan, *Guns and Rain: Guerrillas and Spirit Mediums in Zimbabwe*, London: Currey, 1985.

note that most children with such names belong to the "born-free" generation and their parents are mostly young Christian couples. Can we learn anything about the search for identity behind these names? How is language being used as a tool in this quest? What are the implications for African Christianity?

At first glance, investigation into African naming practices appears to be a mundane undertaking. However, when one realises that the history of Shona nomenclature is inextricably intertwined with both political and religious history of the country, one is bound to be more cautions. The rise of vernacular Christian names is not an accident of history. Indeed, it is a product of history. It testifies to a people's quest for identity. Behind the indigenous Christian name is the cry for identity. Behind the indigenous Christian name is the cry of anguish, a painstaking search for what it means to be both African and Christian or to be Christian and African.

Theology and Language

As we saw, the denial of African names went hand in hand with the trivialization of indigenous languages. Emmanuel Martey notes that language is an important resource for doing theology. He argues, "if language, as we have established, is at the very heart of culture, and if it is impossible for an authentic African cultural revolution to take place using a foreign language, then African writers, including theologians, must take African languages seriously".[19]

Lamin Sanneh's scholarly but controversial work, *Translating the Message*[20] seeks to explode the widely held idea that missionaries were willing pawns in the hands of colonialism and that they were culturally arrogant. He argues, with a great deal of erudition, that missionaries were sympathetic to African language and culture. While Sanneh thesis is brilliant, our own examination of the history of African names in Zimbabwe, at least leads us to be cautious in accepting his revisionist project. Admittedly, we have isolated one facet from the gamut of cultural practices, but as we have endeavoured to demonstrate, it is by no means a peripheral one. While

---

19 E. Martey, *African Theology: Inculturation and Liberation*, Maryknoll: Orbis, 1993, pp. 45f.

20 Lamin Sanneh, *Translating the Message: The Missionary Impact on Culture*, Maryknoll: Orbis, 1989.

mission of translation provides new insights into the history of mission, it is too quick to exonerate the missionaries. According to the Zimbabwe situation, indigenous languages were down-played during the implantation and subsequent growth of Christianity. This may be seen in the widespread practice of adopting English names as we saw above.

The Cameroonian theologian Jean-Marc Ela maintains that to have an "African" name is too superficial an attempt at excavating one's roots. It is a hopeless search for an African mythological past and this return to ancestral names is futile.[21] One may understand Marc-Ela more on this statement when one examines his impatience with African cultural nationalists. His theology focuses on what he regards as the primary task, the liberation of Africa from debilitating economic dependency. Such an urgent undertaking, it would seem for Marc-Ela and other liberationist African theologians, leaves no room for such peripheral issues such as names. However, as J.S. Pobee notes, one needs to be guarded when seeing these efforts as frivolous. Referring to his own 'conversion', he says: "In other words, I am not as sure as I used to be about the distinction between the external and the internal, the accidental and the essential."[22] In the Zimbabwean context, naming practices among youthful couples are not a wholesale return to ancestral names. Names like Munyaradzi (comforter), Tinomudaishe (we love the Lord), Ropafadzo (blessing) and many others are vehicles for expressing the Christian faith.

The names are therefore Shona and Christian. They are a result of the parent's realisation that there is no contradiction between the two. At stake here is not the much-vaunted multiple identity confronting the African Christian. In giving their children indigenous Christian names, most parents are consciously challenging the trivialization of vernacular languages. They have come to realise that local languages can effectively communicate their faith. J.S. Mbiti comments on the history of the implantation of Christianity in Africa thus: "It was very unfortunate, therefore, that Africans were told by word and example, by those who brought them the Gospel, that they first had to become culturally circumcised before they could become Christians".[23]

---

21 Jean-Marc Ela, *African Cry*, Maryknoll: Orbis, 1986, p. 126.

22 J.S. Pobee, Skenosis#, p. 17.

23 J.S. Mbiti, "Christianity and African Culture," *Journal for Theology in Southern Africa*, September 1977, p. 29.

In an investigation into naming trends in Zimbabwe one encounters a quest for identity. The African Christian community in Zimbabwe has largely continued with the practice of *sazita* (naming a child after a relative). However, unlike in the past where such a child would be respected, this is modified. In most instances, if the name of the deceased was an English one, a Shona Christian one is given alongside the English name. It is clear, therefore, that there is a marked affirmation of the possibility and suitability of using indigenous names as an expression of one's Christian faith.

VI. Conclusion

At the first glance it would seem that the issue of names is shifting sand on which to erect a study. However, as we have illustrated, a name in Shona communities is laden with meaning. This becomes clear when we bear in mind the fact that naming practices among African Christians have been indelibly affected by the political and religious history of the country. Instead of glorifying a 'dead African past' by returning to ancestral names, African Christians in Zimbabwe have respected their cultural heritage by insisting on the value of indigenous names to which they have given a Christian colouring. This is their starting point in a long pilgrimage, and in a real sense they are doing theology. Through the names they give to their children, they are reflecting on the implications of what it means to be a Christian in Africa. As such the quest for identity is not the preserve of a few, professional theologians and scholars.

This article has also brought out the extend to which African culture, represented by the denial of culture-bound names, suffered during the colonial period. It is not therefore a historical accident that the arrival of political independence coincided with a rise in vernacular names. The names had and continue to have Christian connotations since, "this Christian movement has been one of the great realities of twentieth century Africa"[24] It is therefore an aspect of African identity. Further research is necessary to establish whether this phenomenon is limited to youthful Christian couples

24 T. Ranger, "Religion, Development and African Christian Identity", in K.H. Petersen (ed.), *Religion, Development and African Identity*, Uppsala: Scandinavian Institute of African Studies, 1987, p. 29.

and whether it is found in the African Independent Churches. A comparative approach which examines the trend amongst African Muslims would also be quite illuminating.

From the discussion above, it becomes clear that continued attempts to argue for and define African Theology are not necessary. In response to the question, "what's in a name?", African Christians in Zimbabwe insist, alongside the traditionalists, that a name radiates and deploys meaning. Through their naming practices, African Christians are engaged in African Theology. This is so if we understand African Theology as J.W.Z. Kurewa does: "Thus African Theology is a theology which comes out of the experience of a people of Africa; it is a theology based on Biblical Faith - a theology which seeks to speak to African communities relevantly and distinctly."[25]

25 J.W.Z. Kurewa, "The Meaning of African Theology", *Journal of Theology for Southern Africa*, July 1975, p. 42.

Slow Cooking: Some European Historical Parallels for the Adaptation of Christianity in Africa

Bruce S. Bennett

Introduction

This is a paper which will stray across the boundaries between history and theology. It attempts to provide some historical background for the theological question of this conference: How is theology to be cooked in an African pot? I suggest that it may help to remember that this is not the first time Christianity has had to become acclimatized in a strange environment. It has been said that until the last few centuries, Christianity was a tribal religion of the Caucasian peoples.[1] Whether or not this is fair, it is remarkable that a religion introduced to Europeans by missionaries had become sufficiently naturalized to seem a badge of Europeanness. The British missionaries who came to Southern Africa were the descendants of peoples who, at the time when the gospel had already spread to Ethiopia,[2] bowed to Odin and Thor.

Analyses of the introduction of Christianity to Southern Africa have tended to be based on a relatively immediate focus: on the one hand, the nineteenth century, capitalist, European background of the missionaries; on the other, the specific societies of the region. I want to suggest that we may benefit also from a very long-term viewpoint, that of the dynamics of Christianity as a world-historical phenomenon.[3] The great organized reli-

---

I wish to thank Dr Shelagh Sneddon and Dr Alasdair Preston of Cambridge for their comments on earlier drafts of this paper.

1 Andrew Walls, quoted in John Parratt, *Reinventing Christianity: African Theology Today*, Grand Rapids: Eerdmans, 1995, p. 1.

2 Stephen Neill, *A History of Christian Missions*, London: Penguin, 1986, p. 47.

3 For some examples of how such a viewpoint can be applied, see Adrian Hastings, *A History of African Christianity 1950-1975*, Cambridge: Cambridge University Press, 1979, pp. 69-73. Hastings suggests, for example, that the advent of African Independent Churches should not be seen purely as a local *reaction* to problems in missionary Christianity, but also as a proactive development, comparable

gions represent collectivities of human endeavour and experience which show remarkable persistence and an essential continuity despite enormous change. At various different times, people have argued that contemporary forces were of such magnitude that they must overwhelm this continuity, yet it has never yet happened thus. The Christian Church has its own dynamics, which the historian must acknowledge. Its time scale is a long one. Even those who see Christianity as facing an unprecedented challenge and likelihood of radical transformation, see such a challenge in terms of intellectual movements starting in the eighteenth or nineteenth centuries; that is, between 250 and 150 years ago, and yet the belief that such challenges will prove fatal is still only conjectural.

Many discussions of the adaptation of Christianity to African conditions contrast the Ancient Greek world-view with the African world-view, as if Christianity had passed directly from one to the other. But in fact, Christianity was brought to Southern Africa by western Europeans, descendants of the peoples who themselves received the original Jewish/Greek Christianity from missionaries. The culture of pre-Christian western Europe was perhaps more closely related to that of ancient Greek and Roman Christians than that of Africa. Nevertheless, Christianity came to north-west Europe as a new, alien religion, which contradicted many aspects of the traditional culture. The situation of Christianity in Africa is by no means as unprecedented as some seem to imagine.[4] Perhaps, by looking at this European[5] process of adaptation, we can learn something relevant to Africa. This paper will look at some examples of how Christianity in Europe interacted with previously-established cultural phenomena. With such a large subject, my approach will be rather eclectic, picking up examples which will, I hope, be suggestive and interesting for African theologians, rather than exhaustive or truly systematic. I will look particularly at Britain.

---

to Protestant church-formation in other Christian contexts and reflecting the familiar Christian pattern of biblically derived criticism of existing structures.

4 For example, consider the complaint that most Christological titles have no resonance for African thought patterns (John Mbiti, quoted in Parratt, *Reinventing Christianity*, pp. 80-1.) It is far from clear that they would have had any more resonance for Europeans when they first heard them.

5 For convenience, I will refer to the north-west European predecessors of the missionaries as Europeans, though strictly speaking that term should include inhabitants of other parts of Europe who were Christianized earlier.

The Old Beliefs

What were the old beliefs which Christianity replaced? Unfortunately, our knowledge of European paganism is much less than could be wished; we have, for example, good information on the stories about the Germanic gods. There was a remarkably complex narrative of their origins, exploits and future demise but much less on how they were worshipped or invoked.[6] These Germanic gods are associated with the Anglo-Saxons who became the dominant group in what is now England; the Celtic Britons whom the Anglo-Saxons gradually displaced, absorbed or subjugated had different traditions. Rituals took place in the open air as well as in temples. The Germanic peoples worshipped, for example, a sky and thunder god Thor, but Odin (Woden to the English) was the king of the gods. He seems to have had connections to shamanism, and is the subject of some strange stories, such as how he hung on the World Tree for nine nights, pierced by a spear, to gain wisdom.[7] In practice, Thor may have been more widely worshipped than Odin. There are some parallels to Christianity, as in the story of Balder the Beautiful who was unjustly killed and (almost) resurrected,[8] but overall the tone of the myths is quite different. Both Germanic and Celtic religions seem to have involved human sacrifice, though it is uncertain how common this was.

What happened to the old gods? At the highest level, they simply disappeared. The myths remained as literary treasures, and a few aspects of them were used for a while in Christian art, but they were definitely excluded from the Christian orthodoxy. At a lower level, however, they lingered, but with declining status. In the shadow of Christian condemnation, some eventually came to be devils.[9] The names of the major gods

---

6 It is interesting to note that in Botswana, some aspects of traditional religious belief which were abandoned are already quite hard to reconstruct. See e.g. I. Schapera & John L. Comaroff, *The Tswana*, rev. ed., London: Kegan Paul, 1991, pp. 53; Paul Stuart Landau, *The Realm of the Word: Language, Gender and Christianity in a Southern African Kingdom*, Portsmouth: Heinemann, 1995, p. 5.

7 This may have paralleled the manner in which human sacrifices were made to Odin.

8 There is a further parallel in his mother Frigg, the weeping Queen of Heaven.

9 Aron Guverich, *Medieval Popular Culture: Problems of Belief and Perception*, trans. János M. Bak & Paul A. Hollingsworth, Cambridge: Cambridge University Press, 1990, p. 84. See C.S. Lewis, *The Discarded Image: An Introduction to Medieval and Renaissance Literature*, Cambridge: Cambridge University Press, 1994 for the process whereby the fairy spirits or elves became demons.

remain in the days of the week; Wednesday is Woden's day Thursday is Thor's day, etc.

Medieval theology about previous religious beliefs varied. Some theologians saw paganism as simply deluded and false. Others, such as Snorri Sturluson, a thirteenth century Icelandic poet and historian who collected and recorded Norse myths, saw the old beliefs as gropings after truth by people who, although they had not yet heard the gospel, nevertheless recognized the existence of God. Still others suggested that the gods were in fact deified ancestors and heroes.[10] This range of approaches to traditional religion: condemnation, acceptance of it as a precursor, and rationalizing analysis seems oddly familiar.

There were other supernatural beings besides the great gods, and some of these lived on in the minds of Europeans. There were for example the Little People, the fairies and elves.[11] These are curiously apart, apparently neither good nor evil, sometimes helpful, but often capricious and dangerous. They live underground and dance in the fields at night. Twentieth-century children's stories have made them pretty and inoffensive, but when they were believed in, they were frightening, beautiful to behold but better avoided. A twentieth-century writer caught their fascination and menace:

> Grizzlebeard: And you .... have you ever seen the Fairies?
>
> Myself: I do not think so .... alas for me! But I think I have heard them once or twice, murmuring and chattering, and pattering and clattering, and flattering and mocking at me, and alluring me onwards towards the perilous edges and the water-ledges where the torrent tumbles and cascades in the high hills.
>
> The Sailor: What did they say to you?
>
> Myself: They told me I should never get home, and I never have.[12]

One of the more sinister activities of the fairies was to steal an infant, leaving an evil, pseudo-human changeling in its place.

---

10 Hilda Ellis Davidson, *The Lost Beliefs of Northern Europe*, London: Routledge, 1993, pp. 144f.

11 See C.S. Lewis, *The Discarded Image*, pp. 122-138. Although fairies have been somewhat standardized in European folklore, they were probably originally part of a much more complex and diverse world of supernatural beings inhabiting nature.

12 Hilaire Belloc, *The Four Men*, Oxford: Oxford University Press, 1984 [1911], p. 55.

Belief in fairies seems to have finally died, but belief in ghosts is still lively.[13] The fear of ghosts, discarnate spirits of the dead, wandering the earth or haunting a place or person remains embedded in European minds, even in resolute rationalists. This fear is interesting in that the ghost is hardly ever supposed to be able to inflict any concrete harm; merely to meet a ghost is somehow deeply horrifying to the European. Ghosts can be fitted into the Christian schema to some extent, as souls which have for some reason not departed from this world, and the ritual of exorcism of ghosts by a priest is still performed.

Many of these motifs appear in European folklore, where they are reduced to stories which no longer challenge Christianity. The same elements, and even the same characters, appear in medieval accounts of superstition and in the folk stories which were recorded hundreds of years later, so there is clearly a continuity.[14] But these elements have transferred from the active category of belief to the hinterland of folklore, things told in stories but not necessarily considered real. Few Europeans now believe in the elves, trolls, or werewolves about which they tell stories. In the case of ghosts, which retain a much higher degree of credibility, it is noticeable that stories about them are more often for adult audiences, and have an anecdotal rather than a fantastic character.

The Arrival of Christianity

Although the Roman Empire had become Christian following the conversion of the emperor Constantine in the early fourth century,[15] Christianity lost ground in the west with the influx of Germanic invaders. Christianity was brought to north-west Europe by missionaries from the south and east. In England, for example, (then divided into a number of kingdoms) the

---

[13] The word ghost originally means spirit, as in Holy Ghost. Early medieval ghosts were not necessarily spirits of the dead. The modern European ghost seems to have become standardized more recently, possibly under the influence of popular understandings of Christian eschatology.

[14] Guverich, *Medieval Popular Culture*, p. 95.

[15] Constantine's conversion is usually dated at AD 312, when he had a vision of the cross superimposed on the sun. As the vision suggests, Constantine at first apparently tried to combine Christianity with his previous allegiance to the cult of *Sol Invictus*, the Unconquered Sun. When in 321 he declared the first day of the week as a holiday, it was declared as Sun-day, the name it still bears in most European languages.

missionary St Augustine of Canterbury arrived in AD 597.[16] There were also missionaries from Ireland, which had been converted earlier. (Ireland could also provide some interesting parallels, for example in the persistence of polygamy in Irish society for several centuries despite Christian condemnation.[17]) The King of Kent (in south-east England) met the visitor in the open air, rather than indoors, as a precaution against the strange magic. He expressed interest, but said that the Christian teachings were new and strange to us, and I cannot accept them and abandon the age-old beliefs of the whole English nation.[18]

However, within a hundred years all the English kingdoms were officially Christian. Conversion was a matter of state policy, not individual choice; when the king converted all his people followed, at least nominally. In a way, therefore, Christianization had to come after conversion. The old beliefs had not simply disappeared. The Church recognized this, and planned for the long term. Pope Gregory I wrote to the missionary Mellitus in 601:

> We have been giving careful thought to the affairs of the English, and have come to the conclusion that the temples of the idols in that country should on no account be destroyed. He [Augustine] is to destroy the idols, but the temples themselves are to be aspersed with holy water, altars set up, and relics enclosed in them .... In this way, we hope that the people .... may resort to these places as before, and may come to know and adore the true God.[19]

Similarly, pagan feasts should not be simply forbidden, but turned into Christian feasts.

> For it is certainly impossible to eradicate all errors from obstinate minds at one stroke, and whoever wishes to climb to a mountain top climbs gradually step by step, and not in one leap.[20]

---

16 There was already a Celtic British church in the west, surviving from before the Anglo-Saxon invasions, but it seems to have regarded any missionary activity toward the ferociously hostile English as impracticable (Neill, *A History of Christian Missions*, p. 58).

17 Hugh Kearney, *The British Isles: A History of Four Nations*, Cambridge: Cambridge University Press, 1995, p. 44.

18 Bede, *A History of the English Church and Nation*, trans. Leo Shirley-Price, Harmondsworth: Penguin, 1955, Vol. I.25, p. 69.

19 *Ibid.*, p. 86.

20 *Ibid.*, p. 87.

This is an excellent summary of the Church's basic strategy. The holy place and the holy occasion would be given a new, Christian, meaning, which would gradually supersede the old. The strength of this was that the old religion lost its separate institutions; it could not survive as a separate entity because its signs had been appropriated by Christianity. However, this cut both ways; the Church could not always be sure that its new meaning was the only one. The strategy allowed many aspects of the old religion to flow into the Christianity of the ordinary people. To some extent the Church accepted this as unavoidable; it was playing a long game. But centuries passed, and still much remained in popular culture that the Church disapproved of.

It may sometimes still be possible to identify places where such a takeover of a holy site has taken place. English churchyards traditionally include yew trees, but the oldest yews are older than the churches, and seem to have had pagan significance.[21] Similarly, some very old churches are built next to holy wells, which may have pre-Christian connections.[22]

The missionaries who came to Africa were aware of this tradition, and sometimes attempted to follow it, but generally in a far more timid manner than their early-medieval forebears, though they did at least follow the precedent of seeking indigenous words for religious concepts.[23] The medieval strategy described differed in intent from the modern theological approach of adaptionism, since the goal was not a restatement of Christianity but a transformation of popular ideas. Nevertheless, the effect could sometimes be the same.

Following the strategy described by Gregory I, the Church often appropriated older festivals. The most famous case of this, of course, is the (earlier) takeover of the Romans Saturnalia by Christmas, which has

---

21 When such ancient yews are uprooted, a skeleton is sometimes found, apparently from a body placed under it when it was a sapling.

22 It has been widely held that holy wells, and water in general, were important in pre-Christian British religion and in pre-Reformation popular piety, but doubts have been expressed about whether significant real connections can be traced: James Rattue, *The Living Stream: Holy Wells in Historical Context*, Rochester: Boydell & Brewer, 1995.

23 The Scottish missionaries David Livingstone and John Mackenzie were both well aware of survivals of Celtic belief in Scottish culture, and envisaged some takeovers of African custom, but neither took the idea very far. Livingstone believed that earlier missionaries had been wrong to condemn initiation schools, but did not try to reverse the policy (David Livingstone, *Missionary Travels and Researches in South Africa*, New York, 1971 [1858], pp. 166f).

retained much of Saturnalias character.[24] In England, Christmas is sometimes known as Yule, which derives from the name of the pagan winter-solstice festival. Mistletoe, which is known to have been sacred in pre-Christian tradition,[25] is traditionally hung in Christmas decorations in houses, but although churches are hung with greenery at Christmas, there is a certain reluctance to allow mistletoe to be included.

Easter takes its name from Eostre, goddess of the dawn and of the spring equinox. The festival, although now thoroughly Christianized, retains pre-Christian symbols of rebirth such as the egg. Modern English Christians like to see this as symbolizing a continuity with what was true in the old religion.

Halloween, by contrast, represents an ancient festival which is only uneaily accommodated by Christianity. Halloween is a time of ghosts, spiits and other aspects of the supernatural and uncanny, which have by this century been largely domesticated to a sort of cathartic game for children.

The Appeal of Christianity

As Paul Landau has suggested, it is insufficient to discuss missionary activity as if it alone could explain conversion. The hearers, or at least some of them, must have had reasons for becoming Christians.[26] In the case of early medieval Europe, rulers often had motivations which we might classify as political.[27] But also, and mixed up with these, were reasons we would classify as religious. Bede, writing in the eighth century, describes in a famous passage the discussions held by King Edwin of Northumbria in 627:

---

24 Saturnalia was a festival of feasting, hilarity, inversions of the normal order, and sexual licence. Medieval celebrations included a Lord of Misrule. Pre-Christian tradition approved over-eating and drunkenness on such occasions, which was a source of some concern to the Church. 25 December was also the date of the festival of *Sol Invictus* (the Invincible Sun).

25 It was revered by the Celtic Druids, and also appears in the Germanic story of Balder the Beautiful who was killed by an arrow of mistletoe, the plant which alone had never promised not to harm him.

26 Landau, *The Realm of the Word*, pp. 132f.

27 It is also worth noting that, as in Southern Africa, missionaries came as representatives of a prestigious culture. Bede records an incident, curiously reminiscent of African missions, in which Wilfrid gained the respect of the South Saxons by demonstrating new techniques of sea-fishing (Bede, *A History of the English Church*, IV.13, p. 223).

> Coifi, the High Priest, ..., [said] .... I frankly admit that, in my experience, the religion that we have hitherto professed seems valueless and powerless. None of your subjects has been more devoted to the service of the gods than myself, yet there are many .... who receive greater honours, and who are more successful in all their undertakings. Now, if the gods had any power, they would surely have favoured myself, who have been more zealous in their service. Therefore, if on examination these new teachings are found to be better and more effectual, let us not hesitate to accept them.

Another of the kings chief men .... went on to say:

> Your Majesty, when we compare the present life of man with that time of which we have no knowledge, it seems to me like the swift flight of a lone sparrow through the banqueting hall where you sit in the winter months to dine with your thanes and counsellors. Inside there is a comforting fire to warm the room; outside, the wintry storms of snow and rain are raging. The sparrow flies swiftly in through one door of the hall, and out through another. While he is inside, he is safe from the winter storms; but after a few moments of comfort, he vanishes from sight into the darkness whence he came. Similarly, man appears on earth for a little while, but we know nothing of what went before this life, and what follows. Therefore if this new teaching can reveal any more certain knowledge, it seems only right that we should follow it.[28]

Although Bede was writing about a hundred years after these events, and his account may be more literary than historical, there is something deeply convincing in this summary of the discussion. Pre-Christian belief did in fact give some answers about the future life, but they were vague and perhaps unsatisfying. Warriors possibly went to join Odin in Valhalla, but in general the dead descended into a shadowy and dismal Niflheim, which may have resembled the ancient Hebrews Sheol.[29] Ancestors do not seem

---

28 Bede, *A History of the English Church*, II.13, pp. 124f.

29 European cultural attitudes to death have varied considerably over time, and vary now within Europe. The late Middle Ages, for example, seem to have been characterized by a rather morbid fascination with the proximity of death, symbolized by the Danse Macabre. (In a window of Bern Cathedral, for example, a party goer looks round and sees that Death, depicted as a skeleton, is playing the lute and putting his hand on his shoulder.) This seems to have begun in reaction to the catastrophe of the Black Death, a plague which killed about a third of the population of Europe in 1348 and which returned periodically for years afterward. Whatever its origins, though, this public and gloating fascination is a long way from present-day British attitudes.

to have the same significance as in African and many other cultures; people apparently appealed to gods, not ancestors.[30]

It is interesting that in Bede's account a noble gives the profound theological allegory, while the priest gives a more prosaic analysis. The allegory of the sparrows flight is still frequently quoted, and apparently expresses something fundamental about the appeal of Christianity to the European mind.

Medieval Christianity

Medieval Europe was a society of two cultures, a popular, oral culture, and a high culture of the written word, accessible only to the literate minority. (In this it has some parallels with modern Africa.[31]) The popular version, especially in rural areas, incorporated huge amounts of pre-Christian content. Although it accepted the new Christian framework, it often gave Christianity different emphases from those of the elite version.

Some scholars have argued, in fact, that medieval Europe was not really a Christian culture at all. By this argument, the Church had never really succeeded in converting the masses, but had imposed a Christian veneer on its culture. It was only with the Reformation and Counter-Reformation that the masses were seriously Christianized. Against this theory, which perhaps takes too rigidly orthodox a view of what can be counted as real Christianity, recent works such as Eamon Duffy's *The Stripping of the Altars* have emphasized the vitality of pre-Reformation, popular Christianity, and shown that although the elite and popular versions may have been different, they were nonetheless coherently connected. (Indeed, in the Middle Ages it may be more accurate to envisage a spectrum of belief, rather than simply a high and low culture.) The question is perhaps one of timing:

---

30 Ancestors may have had some role; our knowledge of household religion, to which such a role might have been relevant, is too sketchy to be certain. The *dísír* of Norse religion may possibly have been female ancestors. (*Encyclopædia Britannica*, 15th ed., vol. 18, p. 900.) Any such role for ancestors seems to have vanished without trace, suggesting that they were much less central than in traditional African belief.

31 Another parallel with modern Africa is that of language. Medieval Europe had many vernacular languages, none of which had high status. The language of learning, including all theology, was Latin, a tongue no longer spoken as a first language, which had to be acquired before one could participate in elite culture. The medieval university was, like the modern African university, a place where all academic discourse was in a second language.

there is little doubt that Christianization was superficial at first but became increasingly real at some time during the middle ages.

A parish Catholicism was the eventual outcome; a Christianity able to link popular and elite interpretations. Some impression of this can still be got from the Catholicism of southern Europe, where festivals often include elements of popular tradition that north Europeans find bizarre, such as throwing a live goat off a church tower, or launching a rocket-propelled stuffed dove from the high altar.[32]

Medieval Christianity placed great emphasis on saints. Saints not only offered an example of the Christian life, they also interceded with God and performed miracles. The relics, physically linking the Christian with the saints presence, were of enormous importance, and great efforts would be made to secure them. Not only were relics bought, sold and stolen, but in the early middle ages there were cases where the option of killing a holy man before he travelled away was contemplated.[33] Miracles were central, and saints could be assessed by the number they had performed. Saints were potent and active; they could heal, but they could also be quick to take offence. In one story, St John the Baptist appeared to a canon in Bonn who had not paid proper respect in a church dedicated to him; the saint did not merely rebuke him but kicked him in the stomach. In another, the Blessed Virgin Mary slapped a nun who was tempted by the endearments of a priest.[34]

Part of the attraction of saints was that they were particular, a patron saint brought benefits for the place or institution which honoured him or kept his relics. The shrine of an important saint such as St Thomas at Canterbury could become a pilgrimage destination, where those helped by the saint came to thank him with prayer and with gifts to the shrine. The particularity of saints is also evident in that they sometimes specialize in particular types of problem; for example St Apollonia helps in cases of toothache. There was a saint for every place, every profession, every occasion. If the life of a saint was not well recorded, the details could be supplied by what seemed likely for such a holy person, leading to such colour-

---

32 These are both real examples.

33 Guverich, *Medieval Popular Culture*, p. 41.

34 Guverich, *Medieval Popular Culture*, p. 202. Not only saints behaved like this; in an even more startling story, a monk who dozed during a vigil was woken when Christ came down from the cross above the altar, and punched him on the jaw (*ibid.*, p. 203).

ful stories as St Ursula and her eleven thousand virgins, St Wilgefortis who was assisted in her vow of chastity by miraculously growing a beard, and St Azenor, one of whose breasts was of gold, and who gave birth to St Budoc while on a five-month sea-voyage in a barrel.

The cult of the saints represents one of the medieval Church's most successful linkages of elite and popular religion. Multiple, flexible understandings could be allowed with the saints, in ways which would not have been acceptable with reference to God. In the early middle ages, this tolerated ambiguity meant that saints sometimes absorbed aspects of pagan deities, allowing such devotions to be gradually Christianized.[35]

The saint was the ultimate popular hero of the medieval world. Whatever ones view of saints who kick sinners in the stomach, this point is worth emphasizing. This exaltation of the world-renouncing holy man represents a notable development of European culture, altering (though not destroying) the pre-Christian emphasis on physical prowess and civic virtue.[36] One of the interesting aspects of medieval culture is the way in which it emphasized the contradictions between the values of this world and those of the next. Depictions of the Last Judgment often showed kings, bishops and even popes among the damned. The ascendancy of the spiritual over the powers of this world was demonstrated by showing the saint as directly, even physically, triumphant.

The particularity of the saints, and the way in which they could absorb pre-Christian devotions, seem to have met a spiritual need for some supernatural patron who would be more local, more specialized, more approachable than the universal God. This may have implications for African theology. Whereas in Europe the need was to find something to meet the need

---

[35] The African-derived syncretist religions of the Americas, such as Santeria, show a comparable syncretism of saints with gods; for example St Barbara, the patron saint against lightning, with Shango the West African god of thunder. However, in medieval Europe, the Church's ultimate control of public articulation of belief led to the Christian identity slowly absorbing the other, which may not be happening in Santeria.

[36] Guverich, *Medieval Popular Culture*, p. 43. The two codes of heroism could overlap, particularly in the early middle ages. Christian kings sometimes became saints, especially if they were martyred, like St Edmund, the King of the East Angles, who was killed in 869 by the invading (and pagan) Danes. Martyrdom could be defined loosely in such cases, as with Edward the Martyr, who was killed for ordinary political reasons in 978, or St Cleodicus (Clydawg), a minor British ruler killed in an *affaire du coeur*. Non-martyred royal saints include Edward the Confessor of England (d. 1066) and Louis IX of France (d. 1270).

formerly met by local gods and spirits, in Africa there is the issue of how the ancestors are to be related to Christianity.[37] I am not suggesting the cult of saints as a direct model, but as an example of how Christianity can incorporate such needs. John V. Taylor, for example, has suggested that the ancestors must somehow be included in the communion of saints of which the Creed speaks.[38] It should be noted that the cult of the saints took a long time to develop, and did so under conditions of high practical tolerance combined with a final insistence on orthodoxy.

Medieval Europe was an agrarian, peasant society, and fertility rituals were importance. The Church provided its own set of rituals, some of which still continue, such as the blessing of the fields on Rogation Sunday, but peasants continued to follow other practices as well. If rain was needed, eleventh-century German peasants might perform a ritual in which a naked girl dug up a certain herb, and was then chased by other girls to a stream.[39] This was condemned as pagan, but sometimes these rituals were blended with Christianity, as in the tenth-century English Æcerbot or Field-Remedy to make a field fertile, in which (among other ceremonies) four symbolic pieces of turf were taken to church, where four masses were said.[40]

One major difference between the European and African cases is of course the division of the Church at the present day. However, medieval Christianity was not completely united. To start with, at the time Christianity came to Europe, there was at least one major rival to the Catholic Church: Arian Christianity. When Clovis, King of the Franks, was converted from paganism to Catholic Christianity in 496, he was the only Catholic Germanic ruler. The Visigoths in Spain, the Ostrogoths in Italy, and the Vandals in North Africa, were all Arian. Even when Arianism had been overcome, unofficial or heretical versions of Christianity kept

---

37 Early missionary attitudes to the veneration of ancestors were negative. John Moffatt, notoriously, tried to equate *badimo* (Tswana ancestors) with evil spirits. In some small Tswana villages, where African ministry was more important than that of the missionary, *badimo* have become identified with angels (Landau, *The Realm of the Word*, p. 93, n. 48).

38 John V. Taylor, *The Primal Vision: Christian Presence amid African Religion*, London: SCM, 1977 [1963], pp. 146-163. Taylor uses an image of the African holding hands with his or her ancestors, and suggests that neither party should be asked to let go. It is noteworthy that one of Sechele's first responses to Livingstones preaching was concern about the position of his ancestors.

39 Guverich, *Medieval Popular Culture*, p. 82.

40 Kathleen Herbert, *Looking for the Lost Gods of England*, Pinner: Anglo-Saxon Books, 1994, pp. 12-15.

appearing. These (perhaps nascent European Independent Churches?) however, were continually suppressed if they became large enough to attract notice. In the early middle ages the suppression was slow, erratic and relatively mild. Later it would become increasingly forceful, culminating in the Inquisition, and events such as the Albigensian Crusade against the Cathars. Unlike in Africa, the Church had access to direct political power to enforce orthodoxy.

Whether or not medieval Europeans were completely Christian, Christianity was the dominant paradigm of thought. Intellectual debate took place within the framework of this paradigm; Theology was the Queen of the Sciences. There was a lack of alternatives to Christianity, in a way which had not been true earlier in the Church's history and would not be true later. Within Europe, the pre-Christian religions were on the way out, and direct mission was no longer necessary (although in some parts of the far north the process of conversion continued into early-modern times). On its borders, however, Christianity could not expand. To the west was the uncrossed Atlantic, and to the south and south-east there was the border with Islam, the rival. No mission was possible there; relations between Christendom and Islam were openly hostile. The Christians gained ground, very slowly, by the reconquest of the Iberian peninsula; attempted less successfully to take the middle east in the Crusades, and eventually lost ground in Asia Minor and the Balkans to the advancing Ottomans. From the east, out of Central Asia, came invaders such as the Mongols on whom the Europeans could make little impression. Thus missionary activity was not generally practical. The concept of Christendom indicates this rather static conception of the Church.

Nevertheless, despite this lack of alternatives in practice, it was possible in principle to conceive of Christianity as a system which could be accepted or not;[41] even within Europe there existed a non-Christian minority, the barely-tolerated Jews. However, the medieval Christian was in no doubt about the choice: The Christians are right, the pagans are wrong.[42] Whether the belief of the Albigensians should be regarded as a Christian

---

41 The anti-hero Reynard the Fox includes in his confession that he has been a perfect heretic and apostate, having denied Christianity (*The Romance of Reynard the Fox*, trans. D.D.R. Owen, Oxford: Oxford University Press, 1994, p. 134). Admittedly Reynard's confession, in which he goes on to propose a system of weekly sex for monks, was mainly a prelude to eating his confessor.

42 *The Song of Roland*, 79 (trans. Dorothy L. Sayers, Harmondsworth: Penguin, 1986, p. 91).

heresy or as a distinct religion is a debatable point; what is certain is that it was ruthlessly attacked as treason to God. Albigensian churches in orthodox towns would have been no more possible than a Pro-Apartheid Society on an African campus.

Medieval Culture

Medieval Europe had a remarkably varied culture in terms of mood. On the one hand, from some sources it seems full of gloom, fear of damnation, and unhealthy horror of sexuality. Yet it was also a culture capable of great gaiety. The medieval story of Reynard the Fox is full of the most extraordinarily vivid humour, sex and violence; a sort of X-rated Tom and Jerry cartoon.[43] The two extremes could co-exist; indeed Guverich suggests that it is this coming together of opposite poles, the grotesque, is peculiarly characteristic of medieval culture. Stories about devils provide an example: medieval Christians were terrified of devils, to an extent we can hardly imagine, yet they could also joke about them. The vitality of medieval Christianity can be seen in the artistic heritage to which it gave rise, above all the immense stone cathedrals with their dizzying perspectives and brilliant stained glass.[44] The medieval Christian lived in a spiritual world of appalling vividness; heaven and hell were both close at hand.

Witchcraft

Witchcraft has an interesting history in Europe. The early medieval Church generally denied the reality of witchcraft. Some people, admittedly, attempted to practise witchcraft, but this was considered sheer delusion. An eleventh-century penitential prescribed a two-year penance for anyone who had believed such things.[45] However, popular belief continued: ordinary people believed in the power of witchcraft and attempted to protect against it by magic.

In the late middle ages, however, official opinion altered to incorporate this aspect of traditional belief. Witchcraft came to be seen as a real and

---

43 I owe this analogy to the Reynard scholar, my friend Dr Jim Simpson of Glasgow University.

44 The cathedrals are also notable, in the context of this article, for their grotesque carvings and gargoyles, strange playful or demonic figures whose significance is disputed.

45 Guverich, *Medieval Popular Culture*, p. 85.

powerful activity, using the power of the Devil. Witches were therefore enemies of God. In the early-modern period, especially the sixteenth and seventeenth centuries, a witch-craze gripped Europe. Alleged witches, the majority being women, were sought out and executed (often by burning) in large numbers. Many aspects of popular supernatural belief became suspect as connected to witchcraft; for example a woman was burnt in Edinburgh in 1576 for consorting with the fairies.[46] The witch-craze eventually abated, and belief in witchcraft faded away.

There is some debate as to how far Europeans actually attempted to practise witchcraft, and whether such practices can be linked to pre-Christian beliefs. The idea of diabolism or Satanism, which has a certain fascination for Europeans, is paradoxically a Christian phenomenon in that it is defined essentially as a sort of anti-Christianity, centring on reversals of Christian holiness such as the Black Mass, and makes little sense out of a Christian frame of reference.[47]

The episode of the witch-craze suggests that incorporation of popular elements is not necessarily always a good thing. Europeans now look back on the witch-craze with revulsion. This historical background is a major cause of European unease with African witchcraft beliefs, probably a more important cause than any general Eurocentric attitudes to African culture and should be appreciated by Africans discussing the issue with Europeans. How far African and European witchcraft beliefs are in fact comparable is another question.

Fate and the Future

It has been suggested that concern over health has been more central to the ideologies of Africa than to those of other continents,[48] perhaps reflecting the relatively dangerous heath environment. European thought shows a comparable pre-occupation with fate and the future, which is rooted in the pre-Christian cultures of the region. The ideas involved are not entirely consistent,[49] but there is a general sense that the future is partly, but not

---

46 Lewis, *Discarded Image*, p. 124.

47 There have been recent claims, especially by some Evangelical groups, that such activities are widespread and include abuse of children.

48 John Iliffe, *Africans: The History of a Continent*, Cambridge: CUP, 1995, p. 4.

49 There may be a further parallel with African beliefs here. John Iliffe goes on to suggest that

necessarily completely, determined. The future may be foretold by dreams or magic, but such foretelling may sometimes enable one to avoid dangers and thus alter one's future. In its strongest form, one's Fate, Destiny, or Doom, such predetermination is unavoidable, at least in its important aspects. In the ancient world, fate was personified as three sisters who determined everyone's destiny. In the Norse myths fate may be something more impersonal, something grim and remorseless against which no-one can triumph. Even the Norse gods, according to the myths, were doomed to final catastrophe and destruction in Ragnarök, the Twilight of the Gods. Among educated medieval Europeans the concept took the form of Fortune, a personified force which turned the wheel of chance, bringing some up, and putting others down, defeating all attempts to manage ones destiny. The medieval philosophy of history was that the race is not to the swift, nor the battle to the strong, nor yet bread to the wise, nor yet riches to men of understanding, nor yet favour to men of skill; but time and chance happeneth to them all.[50]

Early medieval European people had a continuing interest in foreseeing the future, despite the Church's strong disapproval. A great variety of techniques were used. Around the winter solstice, people would sit on the roof or at a crossroads (locations symbolic of seeing far) or peer into the fire, in order to see the future.[51] If seen, it could perhaps be averted. Rituals could be performed over a corpse. Omens, such as the direction in which a bird flew, could tell you what would happen.[52] Such beliefs have continued into modern times in some parts of Europe.[53]

A more day-to-day form of the same phenomenon is to be found in the European preoccupation with luck. Whether good or bad things happen follows a trend or pattern of good or bad luck. This luck is a curiously impersonal and arbitrary force, which can nevertheless be controlled to some extent. Particular events and behaviours bring good or bad luck. For example, to

---

Africans tended to apply empirical criteria to ritual practices; what was wanted was not so much consistency with some schema but the belief that they *worked* (*ibid.*, p. 87). This seems to be the attitude of Europeans to the sources of good and bad luck.

50 Ecclesiastes 9:11 (AV).

51 Guverich, *Medieval Popular Culture*, p. 82.

52 Guverich, *Medieval Popular Culture*, pp. 88f. This type of omen is known to have had an important place in pre-Christian religion.

53 See Eugenie Fraser, *The House by the Dvina: A Russian Childhood*, London: Corgi, 1995, p. 146 for a traditional Russian ceremony, performed at homes at Epiphany, to foresee the future.

spill salt is unlucky; to do so would generate bad luck which would lead to something unfortunate happening to you. In this case the bad luck can be averted by throwing a pinch of salt over your shoulder. In most cases, there is no answer to the question, why is it unlucky? not only a lack of reasons to identify a particular action as unlucky, but a lack of any intelligible theory as to why any such action should be unlucky. It is not, for example, postulated that God is displeased by spilling salt.[54] One possible explanation is that the system of luck represents part of a pre-Christian religious system; not so much the survival of particular customs (though some such beliefs may have pagan origins) as the persistence of a habit of thought.

It is noteworthy that such patterns tend to surface when Europeans are under stress, even among people who normally discount such ideas. In the war film Memphis Belle, the story concerns a bomber crew on a dangerous mission. At one point, one of the men thinks he has lost his medallion (a representation of a Catholic saint) and starts to panic. To calm him, a comrade gives him his lucky rubber band which he puts around his wrist. Two points should be noted here. The first is the fact that the medallion, an orthodox Catholic symbol, is apparently equated with a random lucky object. Both bring luck; how, evidently is not an issue. The second is that this incident is not humorous. At most times modern Europeans might laugh at the lucky rubber band, but in the airmen's situation of terrible danger, with sudden unpredictable death near at hand, their clutching at luck seems unsurprising, and the viewer does not laugh. Situations of danger or stress seem to encourage such interest in what will bring luck: for example sailors had many powerful superstitions.[55]

The variety of lucky and unlucky things is enormous. Even for Europeans who think they do not take them seriously, such ideas can be embedded in common customs or sayings. It is widely thought to be very unlucky to say anything that presumes success before the issue is decided; for example, to say I am doing well in the exams before they are finished. This

---

54 Some such beliefs do have Christian implications, although they are popular beliefs, not endorsed by the Church. For example, Friday is unlucky because it was the day Christ was crucified. Thirteen is unlucky (especially as the number at table) because it was the number present at the Last Supper. One might have expected the Last Supper to be positive, but the popular idea focussed not on the institution of the sacrament but on the presence of Judas as the thirteenth.

55 One of my own nineteenth-century ancestors recorded in his diary how, on a sailing ship bound for New Zealand, when the ship was becalmed the sailors believed that it was due to the presence of a man who had abandoned his wife. They proposed, apparently quite seriously, to maroon him.

is tempting fate and makes it more likely that something will go wrong. If such a statement is made, the speaker should touch wood, or at least say the words "touch wood"; this will avert the bad luck. This practice is still extremely common even among those who dismiss ideas of luck.[56]

The popularity of astrology in western culture reflects these ideas about the future: the stars are supposed to predict, not exactly what will happen, but what is likely to happen. By knowing this, one can improve ones chances of a good outcome. Medieval Christianity did not reject astrology outright; it was acceptable to believe that the stars had an influence on events and personality, such influence being a natural phenomenon not necessarily of any greater theological significance than other environmental influences.[57] In practice belief in the stars' influence and predictive power tended to go beyond this:

> .... for certainly
> The death of every man is there to see
> Patterned in stars clearer than in a glass
> Could one but read how all will come to pass.[58]

New systems of astrology and prediction, imported from other cultures (such as Chinese astrology) or simply invented, find ready acceptance in the west, because they fit into an already-established habit of thought. Similarly, the frontier Boers in South Africa consulted African traditional doctors about the future;[59] apparently they were ready to accept this aspect of the traditional doctor's work, although, for example, they were unlikely to ask him to make rain.

Although this interest in the future has some connections with the Jewish and Christian concepts of time, it also has significant differences. Popular

---

56 The tendency to develop rituals of reassurance in stressful situations may have a universal dimension. Behaviourist psychologist Skinner claimed to have induced superstitions in pigeons by rewarding behaviour randomly. However, the rationalization of such rituals as *lucky* is a more culturally specific phenomenon.

57 Lewis, *Discarded Image*, pp. 103-9. Medieval Christian attitudes varied somewhat over time.

58 Geoffrey Chaucer, *The Canterbury Tales*, trans. Nevill Coghill, London: Penguin, 1977, p. 144 (The Man of Laws Tale, part I).

59 See e.g. John Mackenzie, *Ten Years North of the Orange River: A Story of Everyday Life and Work among the South African Tribes from 1859-1869*, 2nd ed., London, 1971; first published 1871, p. 52. The practice is referred to in the work of Herman Charles Bosman, e.g. Yellow Moepels, in *Mafeking Road*, Cape Town: Human & Rousseau, 1971.

European understandings of what a prophet is, for example, have focussed on prediction: in everyday English, prophecy simply means prediction. While authentic prophecy is concerned with recalling the hearer to responsibility, ideas of fate can easily lead to a rejection of responsibility.[60] The time of European culture is not exactly the same as the time of Christian eschatology and salvation-history, a point worth bearing in mind when considering how Christian theology can relate to the time of African culture.[61]

To summarize: in spite of the importance of these ideas, fate and luck were never significantly incorporated into the theology of European Christianity,[62] although the common people appropriated some aspects of official Christianity for the system of luck, such as holy medals. Here we see a case where the Christian Church refused to accommodate European habits of thought, even though these habits have not thereby been extirpated.

It is interesting to note that many of the criticisms Europeans made of traditional African society superstition, cruelty, irrationality were the same criticisms they made of their own medieval ancestors. Medieval has in most contexts been a term of abuse. These attitudes have been persistent among non-specialists: a generally very good basic history textbook published in 1978 describes a sixth-century book as filled with outrageous and silly miracles, and states that the sixth-century world was dominated by savage cruelty and beclouded by superstitious fantasy.[63] It is perhaps only with the rise of more tolerant attitudes toward other present-day cultures that most Europeans have begun to appreciate medieval culture as different rather than simply inferior.

Conclusions

The medieval Church, like the modern African Church, had to operate in an environment where popular culture was by no means always in accordance with the new ideas. Overall its approach can be summed up as great

---

60 Indirectly, such attitudes have been involved in movements such as scientific racism which have sought to deny responsibility by appealing to some inevitable biological or historical process.

61 As in the work of John Mbiti.

62 The Calvinist doctrine of predestination may owe something to European ideas of the future, but I would argue that it has a rather different character. In any case, predestination has fallen out of favour in Europe, even in churches with an historically Calvinist background.

63 C. Warren Hollister, *Medieval Europe: A Short History*, New York: John Wiley, [4]1978, p. 41.

tolerance in practice, and in the short-term, but low tolerance in theory, and in the long term. In the short term, which for the medieval Church could be hundreds of years, it was inevitable that ordinary people would continue to follow old habits of thought, and the Church was ready to arrange an easy transition by retaining selected elements of the old ways. But the theologians never deliberately cultivated a European theology. Some modern African Christians have spoken of a sense of a split between their African culture and their Christianity: for example Kenneth Kaunda described a tension created by the collision of two world-views, which I have never completely reconciled.[64] Such an experience would have been quite familiar to the early medieval peasant, had he put it into words. But the medieval Church saw its duty not as being to reconcile the world-views, but to secure the triumph of one over the other.

To some extent, it succeeded. The fact that, as I remarked earlier, present-day writers contrast the Ancient Greek world-view with the African world-view, as if Christianity had passed directly from one to the other, must be taken as evidence that they did. But background belief can be very subtle. As Rabbi Lionel Blue wrote, comparing different traditions within Judaism:

> I realized that Jews had not lived on the moon, and had been more influenced by their surroundings than they cared to acknowledge. The Authentic Judaism of my childhood years was Orthodox, and suspiciously like the Orthodox Church in its attitudes, with the same mixture of long liturgy, warm piety, and a heady combination of saintliness, dottiness and superstition. The resemblance was hardly surprising because we all crept out of the same marshes in White Russia.[65]

It is one thing to exclude a specific belief, another to exclude a way of believing. This is important because it is the adaptation to ways of believing that is most often the goal of African theologians seeking an African theology. An adaptionist European theology may not have been deliberately sought, but to some extent it happened anyway, very slowly. The most successful adaptations, in Europe, reflect a combination of great

---

64 Quoted in John Parratt, *Reinventing Christianity*, p. 14.

65 Lionel Blue, *A Backdoor to Heaven*, London: Fount, 1985, pp. 57f. Rabbi Blue (a prominent rabbi of the Reformed Jewish community in Britain) goes on to show cultural similarities between German Judaism and German Protestantism.

practical tolerance with a theological insistence on orthodoxy, over a long time-span.

Possibly this may be the best way to find such adaptions, through slow imperceptible interaction. But the situation of the Church in modern Africa is different. For one thing, the medieval Church had a secure monopoly; the modern African Church exists in a situation of pluralism and competition. For another, the world of medieval Europe, although not static, changed much less rapidly or dramatically than that of modern Africa.

In the case of European theology, I suspect that the greatest cultural adaptations, in official theology as opposed to popular practice, came much later than the period of Christianity's arrival in Europe. The European culture which modern African theologians seek to disentangle from Christianity is a culture of (for example) individualism, and mechanistic concepts of the world. But these are hardly aspects of the pre-Christian culture of Europe; their roots are to be sought in what has happened to Europe since that time; that is, in the context of an officially Christian society, even if these developments are not especially Christian.

Another point to note is that caution must be exercised when considering the links between Christianity and European culture. While the example of Europe shows examples of Christianity adapting to existing cultures, it also shows examples of resistance to such adaptation, and of cultural elements which have either been displaced by Christianity (such as Irish polygamy) or which have continued to exist uneasily beside it.

The example of Europe can, I suggest, provide a useful background for comparison; an awareness of precedents. It is, however, a source to be used with care and does not provide many easy lessons for those seeking to cook their theology in an African pot, except that it may take a very long time; that some tough bits will eventually boil down into the soup, but that some may never do so; and that it is valid, and perhaps sometimes necessary, to live with unresolved questions. I conclude with a quotation from C. S. Lewis' last novel, *Till We Have Faces*, a neglected and profound book about (among other things) the reconciliation of different sorts of truth:

> Only this I know. This age of ours will one day be the distant past. And the Divine Nature *can* change the past. Nothing is yet in its true form.[66]

---

66 C.S. Lewis, *Till We Have Faces*, London: Fount, 1978, p. 316.

Christianity in a New Context: Specific Cases of Interaction

Saroj N. Parratt

Introduction

"Theology cooked in an African pot" is our theme. The phrase gives the impression that one can put anything (even British beef) in the African tripod steel cooking pot, and what comes out will be African. When Christianity arrived in Africa, and in Botswana in particular, it came with a western wrapping. Christianity went into the pot without being unwrapped. There was no period of observation first. But the pot, Botswana, was not quite empty. Some of what was there was pushed out, some remained and was included in the stew.

The original cooks, the missionaries, expected that, given time, the Africans would become not only Christian but would also adapt to many elements of British culture. However, this is now seen as a mistaken ideal. Africans want the meal, but not the indigestible wrapping which should not have been included. To some extent, the meat has not been cooked properly because it is still sealed in the wrapping.

Interaction

To move away from the metaphor African Christians began to ask, "Who is Christ in the African context?" The essential question is one of interaction. What happened in Botswana was not totally unique, and I am going to compare another interaction, in a different cultural context, which may nevertheless prove illuminating. After examining this historical case, I will move on to look at some specific examples in modern Botswana. The historical example I am using is that of the reform of Hinduism in Bengal in the late eighteenth century, following interaction with Christianity.

In the Bengal case, it was not a reform imposed by political leaders but one carried out by religious leaders influenced by the Enlightenment as well as Christianity. This reformation, in Hinduism, may be described as a "Bengal Renaissance". It included both religious and social aspects. On the religious side, it addressed such issues as the concept of God, how God is to be worshipped, and inter-faith relations and worship. On the social side, it addressed the caste system, *sati* (burning alive of widows on the husband's funeral pyre), the rule that widows (who had not been burnt) could not remarry, child marriage, and polygamy. It is these social aspects which I will address, especially those which affected women, and I will relate the reform movement to questions of social issues of African women, and of Botswana in particular.

After dealing with the social issues, I will try to address the position of women in the church in urban Botswana as the church plays an important part in women's lives, remembering that women have both social and spiritual needs.

Cases of Interaction

Old culture with new religion, new religion with old culture.

It might be argued that the two cases are different, the Indian case is about how old culture is altered by new religion, the African case is about how new religion can be altered by old culture. (Thus the first case is "cooking India in a Christian pot".) However, both cases involve an old and a new culture, mixed and interacting in highly complex ways. In one the dominant system of ideas, or paradigm,[1] was that of the old religion (Hinduism) and in the other the dominant organizing system is that of the new (Christianity). This is a valid point to note, but it does not mean the two cases are incomparable. (Distinguishing paradigm and the material organized; e.g., some African independent churches, at the extreme, use the organizing categories of Christianity; church, minister, God, sacrament; but the content may be more dominated by traditional elements such as ancestors, medicine, sacrifice etc).

In both cases we have two cultures, interacting. Let us put aside for a moment which paradigm is the one officially considered the dominant one,

---

1 The term "paradigm" is used here in Kuhn's history-of-science sense, meaning an over - arching system of ideas which organizes the data. In theology the term is now sometimes used in the rather different sense of an exemplar.

and see what is happening in the actual interaction of ideas. It should not be conceived of as a dilution of Christianity, i.e., African Christianity is not something halfway between received Christianity and African culture. African culture is not a static given which is mixed into a static given Christianity. Both are dynamic systems; we want a development which is a valid development of both. Change is not necessarily about African culture becoming less African. Such a change is of course possible, but there is another sort of change. European western culture has itself changed greatly in the past hundred years, but it has not thereby become "less western", in fact it is often these recent developments of western culture which seem to have the most impact on other cultures.

Indian reformers made changes these changes constitute, indirectly, an answer to their question "Who is Christ?" Thus, doing theology in one's own culture can involve analysis and reform of one's own culture.

The Bengal Renaissance: Change in Indian women's status

The leading figures of this movement were Raja Ram Moan Roy (1772-1833) and Keshab Chandra Sen (1838-1884). Both were influenced by the teaching of Jesus as they read it in the Gospels; although neither became a Christian, in the Church's terms,[2] their reforms reflected these teachings. The social reformation brought a drastic change in the practices and customs of the Hindus of that time.

Roy's first contact with Christianity came entirely by accident. It was his employer and teacher John Digby of the East India Company who, while helping Roy to improve his knowledge of English, introduced him to English literature. According to Mueller, "originally [Roy] had only hatred for the English; but .... his intercourse with Digby and .... study of English literature, led to a change of feeling and conviction".[3] With this change of attitude, Roy made contact with Christian missionaries at Serampore.[4] Out of a combination of contacts with Digby, Christian mis-

---

2 Hinduism is inclusive in nature, and a Hindu would not see it as necessary to give up the religion of his birth in order to accept a new faith. Thus for these reformers, the question of whether they were "Christians" as opposed to Hindus would not have seemed very meaningful. This is relevant to the question, discussed below, of "Who owns Christ?"

3 Quoted in J.N. Farquhar, *Modern Religious Movements in India*, Delhi: Munshiram Manohar Lal Publishers, 1967, p. 31.

4 William Carey arrived in Calcutta in 1793, and started the Serampore Mission in 1800. Roy

sionaries and reading of English literature, Roy was led to the teaching of Jesus in the New Testament. His interest was so keen that he studied Hebrew and Greek in order to read the Bible in the original, and in order to give practical effect to his convictions, he published a remarkable book: *The Principles of Jesus: The Guide to Peace and Happiness*. He wrote in the preface:

> This simple code of religion and morality is so admittedly calculated to elevate Man's ideas to higher and liberal notions of one God and is also so well fitted to regulate the conduct of the human race in the discharge of various duties to God, to themselves, and to society, that I cannot but hope the best effects from its promulgation in the present form.[5]

Roy saw in Jesus a living theism and also the answer to the social problem, and in particular to those of the Hindu family system. It was especially the wrongs of women which stirred him. With conviction he now denounced and condemned *sati* and polygamy, and pleaded for the return of earlier practices by which women had rights of inheritance.

Sati was practised among the royalty, upper classes, and certain castes; the widow had no choice. She was burnt alive on the funeral pyre along with the body of her dead husband. In many cases the widows were quite young, as it was normal practice for an old king or nobleman to marry young girls as junior wives. (Thus there was a link between *sati* and polygamy, though not in all cases). The widow had no chance against the pressures of family and community. Her cries and screams were drowned by the beating of drums and cymbals, while her body was slowly charred by the flames. It was cruel, but it was the custom.

Roy himself took part in agitation against *sati*. On 4 December 1829, Lord Bentinck, the then Governor-General of India, issued an order forbidding *sati*. This has often been seen as the British government intervening to abolish a tradition; but in fact the lead came from Roy and his initially small group of followers, who educated the public. The law followed a public movement from within Indian society. The government agreed with the reformers and implemented their policy, but did not act alone.

---

translated the New Testament into Bengali.

5 Farquhar, *Modern Religious Movements in India*, p. 32.

Roy's social policies were launched from the context of the new religious movement he founded, the Amitya Sabha (Friendly Association) later named Brahma Samaj (Association of Believers in Brahma). In this association men and women of any faith were welcome, as long as God was worshipped.

Roy identified the caste system, polygamy, women's inheritance and *sati* as evils. He lived long enough to see the abolition of *sati*, but it was his successors, including Sen, who had to continue with the other issues, and identified other problems such as polygamy, child marriage, and widow remarriage.

Sen put the question, "India asks: Who is Christ?" in 1879, in a public lecture. This is the same question which Africa has been asking for some time.[6] From this question, African theologians have developed several theologies: African theology, Black theology, etc., and are still trying to relate Christ to the African context.

Roy did not openly ask this question, but saw Christ, and what Christ was saying, as the answer to India's problems, and sought to address India's needs thereby. Sen went further, and spoke directly about what he found in Christ. He appealed to both Asia and Europe to take note of the glorious character of Christ. He was also led to a sense of sin, and its consequences, and the work of the Spirit. He put most emphasis on Christian social attitudes, but this was derived from his experience of Christ through the Holy Spirit. Sen viewed social problems from a spiritual standpoint; social progress followed from spiritual progress. However, spiritual progress also depended on social progress; only in a reformed society could a purer (theistic) religion be established. A major part of this reform would be an improvement in the status of women, and this movement derived its vision from the interaction with Christianity.

The caste system was not legally abolished until independence in 1947, but in practice these followers of the Brahma Samaj disregarded caste. In the removal of any social evil, we should note the difference between legal prohibition and the actual abandonment or absence of the practice. It is the latter, of course, which is really important. Even before legal abolition,

---

6 Around 1706 Kimpa Vita taught that Jesus was an African and that the Black Christ would return to establish a paradise on earth and restore the old Congolese kingdom to its former glory (J. Parratt, *Reinventing Christianity*, Eerdmans: Cambridge, 1995, p. 4).

inter-caste marriage became relatively common, showing the influence of the reform movement in practice.

Women, in the old system, had no place except in the house, and even there only in the kitchen, but as a result of reforms, they gained a place in social gatherings, schools and colleges, and could express opinions. Such drastic changes were made possible by Sen and the other young reformers, putting reforms into practice in their own homes. It was not just a matter of resolutions of committees; they acted on their principles in their own households.

The reformers opposed and ceased to practise polygamy and child marriage. Polygamy disappeared due to a change of attitudes on the part of men. In child marriage, although both a boy and a girl were involved, it was the girl who suffered most. At marriage (perhaps at the age of five and upwards) she moved to the boy's household, where she grew up. The boy would grow up in the normal way, going to school etc., but the girl merely waited until she was of age to consummate the marriage. She had no life of her own, her destiny was already determined and there was no way she could seek her true self. Sometimes a girl was married to an old man; in which case, because of his age, she faced *sati* within a short space of time.

Widow remarriage, which had previously been forbidden, was introduced. This implied an abandonment of the idea of a tie which continued after the husband's death. The widow no longer had to wait in isolation for her death, but could interact in society, and fulfil her life as a woman and a human being.

By the abolition of child marriage and polygamy, and the permitting of widow remarriage, the reformers restored to women the equal status of which previous tradition had robbed them. Thus they put into practice Paul's dictum; "There is neither Jew nor Greek, there is neither slave nor free, there is neither male nor female, for you are all one in Christ Jesus" (Gal. 3:28, RSV). The lower status of women, dated from the Brahmanic period, and also from Muslim influence from the Mughal period. Now, miraculously, they experienced a resurrection. They became human beings with value and dignity.

Bengal situation - African situation. How does this Reformation relate to Africa, and the situation of African women?

This is a task which will have to be done mainly by African women. To start with, it raises the question of who is going to take up the task of seeking what Christianity offers, and how to implement it. In the Indian case, it was the men who led and implemented the initial changes. In the African context, who will do it, and how is it to be done? Should we begin by theologizing, on the classical approach or naturally on the Liberation theology approach? Or do we put into practice first and let theology follow eventually?

The situation of modern African women is, of course, less completely helpless than that of the Indian women before reforms. Thus while in India it was perhaps inevitable that reform, to come at all, had to start with men, in Africa it is more possible for women to start reform themselves. However, this does not mean that men have no role, or no responsibility, or that these problems can be solved without men taking part. Nor, of course, are Africa's social problems the same as those of India. But there are social problems everywhere, and the Christian gospel is of universal application, and so we should be able to learn from the Indian experience. There is no society, "traditional" or "modern", without social problems. We are not yet in a state of fully realized eschatology.

In the case of Africa, and in particular Botswana, on which I am focusing, there are problems in the position of women in society. These problems cannot be made to disappear by ignoring them, or answering complaints with "Is there a problem?" Instead of looking for a let-out, is it not time that Africans, and Tswana men of the Church in particular, face the issues. I say men in particular because in Botswana the leaders of the Church are overwhelmingly men. The majority of Church members may be women, but the decision-makers are men. If, in India, two men who were not even officially Christians were able to take the teaching of Jesus and begin a reformation of a non-Christian society on its basis, why is it not possible for Christian men, in a largely Christian Africa to do the same?

An African theology will take account of the question, "Who is Christ?" and address the condition of women; it is not necessarily a matter of importing western feminism, but about African women: perhaps an "indigenous feminism"? Western feminism is a particular cultural phenomenon which of course addresses some of the same questions, not necessarily exactly the same ones, since it is a response within a particular (western) culture to a set of particular needs. African feminism will undoubtedly have things in common as there are common factors and perhaps some human universals about men and women, however, it should be a response within this culture to the needs of these women.

There have, in fact, been some African women theologians. Therese Souga, for example, equates the lot of African women, in their exclusion, weakness, silence and bearing of burdens with the marginalized women in the gospels. Women "incarnate the suffering of the African people".[7] Louise Tappa sees Jesus as the overcomer of taboos, and Anne Nasimuyu-Wasike writes of Jesus' role as women's hope, refuge, strength and comforter in their position of hardship, marginalization, and burden-bearing in homes, society and church. She sees Jesus as Mother, the nourisher and healer. These theologians see men and women as complementary, and not antagonistic in the manner of some western feminists. They identify the cause of women's suffering in systems. Men should join in changing these systems. Their perspectives range from the practical and realistic to the philosophical and mystical, showing the broad significance of a female perspective in African theology.

This is a difficult area, since the African need to counter racial and colonial oppression has led to a reluctance to consider other oppressions, and the need to protect African culture has led to a reluctance to admit that it may include problems which need reform.

Possible areas needing reformation

Let us take the example of women in Botswana. My comments are based on further analysis on my earlier research on women and development, and women and religious change.[8]

---

7 J. Parratt, *Reinventing Christianity*, p. 90.

8 Saroj N. Parratt, "The Status of Women and Issues in Development in Botswana", in Isabel Phiri, Kenneth Ross, James Cox (eds), *The Role of Christianity in Development, Peace and Reconstruction. Southern Perspectives*, Nairobi: AACC, 1996, pp. 140-155; Saroj N. Parratt, "Religious Change among Women in Urban Botswana", *Journal of Religion in Africa*, vol. XXV, no. 1, 1995, pp. 73-84.

Women in relation to marriage and family

First let us consider marriage. In the west, 'marriage' is a clearly-defined legal status. Although Botswana law (both common and customary) defines marriage, couples (living together, or even apart) will often describe themselves, and be described, as 'married', without any formalities having been observed. Leaving aside legal categories, marriage in Botswana takes three forms: traditional, traditional plus church wedding, and civil. Although the missionaries sought to abolish *bogadi* (bride price paid in cattle), and it was made illegal by several chiefs including Khama III, it has either survived or subsequently revived. In the case of the BaKgatla, the practice was abolished by Linchwe, but restored by Isang on the grounds that it was necessary to stabilize marriage. The Dutch Reformed Church (the mission in Mochudi) accepted this and made *bogadi* a regular element of church marriage, and other churches have since adopted the same policy in the case of people from backgrounds where *bogadi* was traditionally required.[9]

Thus, church marriage often remains within the traditional system. There will be a public church service, which closely resembles the current western church marriage ceremony, including an exchange of vows, and stylistic elements such as the bridal gowns. However, this service cannot take place until *bogadi* is paid, and it is therefore arguable that *bogadi*, rather than the vows, is the essential element. The expense of a wedding is now greatly increased, as it includes not only *bogadi* but also the gown, a large, elaborate and western-style reception, etc. This is a burden that many cannot afford; and yet if all this is not done, many young Tswana will not consider themselves properly married. Inevitably, a common result is that they do not marry at all, or defer formal marriage, until they have sufficient resources. Often this day never arrives. Of course there are many other reasons, but informants do mention expense as a problem.[10] (There is now the possibility of getting a loan for marriage expenses, but couples may already have financial commitments.) Such unmarried couples do not

---

9 Tswana culture generally requires *bogadi* (although there can be exceptions), but some other cultures in Botswana do not. *Bogadi* is not paid all at once, but in instalments, which helps to keep the husband in a state of indebtedness to the wife's family.

10 The BaLete of Ramotswa require not only *bogadi*, but that the husband should have a house of his own. He cannot take his wife to live in his parent's house, although he is allowed to live with the wife's parents (Dr L. Nthoi, personal communication).

perceive themselves as bound, and are much more likely to split up. The end result is a large number of single mothers.[11]

According to the 1991 census the population is 1,326,796; 634,400 males and 692,396 female. Thus 52.19% are women, though in the cities males outnumber women. Of the total population, non-citizens number 29,557: 17,995 male and 11,562 female, constituting 2.84% of total male population and 1.55% of total female population.

So far no figure for the number of single mothers has appeared from the last census. But the break down of women into categories as the census indicates, will be of help to understanding the conditions women are in.

Total number of women aged 12 years and over (who could become mothers, but each is not necessarily a mother) is 457,165. And the total number of children born to them is 1,264,035.

Total number of women who are never married is 252,932 (55.32%) of total number of women of the same age, have 303,445 (24%) of total number of children ever born.

Total number of women who are either separated or divorced is 9,808, (2.15%) of total number of women of the same age, have 466,58 (3.69%) of total number of children ever born .

Total number of women who are widowed is 3,4036 (7.45%) of total number of women of the same age, have 192,532 (15.23%) of total number of children ever born.

Total number of women living together is 48,420 (10.59%) of total number of women of the same age have 165,239 (13.07%) of total children,ever born.

Total number of women whose marital status is not stated is 1,863 (.41%) of total number of women of the same age, have 2,007 (.16%) of total children, ever born.

Total number of women who are married is 110,379 (24.14%) of total number of women of the same age, have 554,154 (43.84%) of total children ever born.[12]

---

11 Figures from the 1991 census show that of Tswana with living mothers, 43.1% have a mother who is either separated, divorced, widowed or never married. Since this includes many older people, the figure for children at the present day is probably much higher. The data I need are not available, so this is an inference from what there is, but a reasonable one.

12 Source: CSO, Analytical report 1991, unpublished tables.

In each of the above case there is no way of knowing whether each woman is a mother. But the above breakdown of information gives us a very clear picture of women in relation to marriage and family.

Unmarried mothers fall mainly into five categories:

(1) Teenagers who engage in sex, and get pregnant, out of peer pressure.
(2) Women who have a child with a man with whom she expected to live, but who was let down. In some cases, this is because the couple simply splits up, in others, a woman is promised marriage once she has proved fertile.
(3) Women who deliberately get pregnant with the aim of persuading their partners to marry them.
(4) Women who decide to have a child although single, and not intending to marry.
(5) Women living with a man although not formally married, and hoping to be married eventually. These women are unmarried but not single mothers.

The chances of women in the first two categories (which includes teenagers) getting married are much less on account of their having had children. According to some men, their faithfulness and trustworthiness are under question, forgetting that men were involved in producing those children born to them. They are judged and condemned. Fortunately, some men are more tolerant and marry women in this category. There was more acceptance of such children in the past as both the woman and her children belonged to the man who paid the *bogadi*. Nonetheless, as most men dream of the ideal, the only alternative left to a majority of such women, if they are to fulfill themselves as women, is that of becoming concubine.[13]

As a concubine a woman may be with one man for a long period, in which case there will be some degree of stability both for her and her child or children. Alternatively, she may become a concubine to a number of men, one after the other.[14] This latter case is more common and it not only produces an unstable atmosphere but even mental disturbance.

Women in the last category (living with a man) do not like to be thought of as "unmarried", but their condition is in fact different from formally

---

13 Sometimes known as a "common law wife".

14 Informants state that in some cases a woman may be a concubine to more than one man at a time.

married couples. Such informal unions may lead to formal marriage as they hope, but may not, and until that point the woman is in fact insecure. Part of their reason for saying they are not "unmarried" is that traditionally, marriage did not take place at one moment, but was the outcome of a process of family interaction etc. Thus they are in the process of "getting married". However, the traditional process had the backing of the two families, and was very unlikely to leave the woman and children stranded halfway. In the present day, this is a real possibility, partly because, among other factors, the process has become so much longer and more expensive. The view that the requirement for traditional and church marriage is a major cause of this, cannot altogether be ruled out. [15]

Here I wish to draw a comparison with the Bengal reformers. The traditional Hindu wedding was extremely elaborate and expensive, and involved not only the couple but gods, ancestors. and a large dowry. The reformers introduced a simple ceremony, in which vows by the couple became the essence of the marriage. This implied a modified concept of what a marriage is. The reformers saw it as focussed on the couple, and their vows. This implied personal consent and contract, and implicitly excluded child marriage. This concept of marriage was taken from Christianity, but they did not adopt western trappings such as gowns or receptions. They adopted an idea, not a fashion. The new type of wedding was recognized by statute in 1872, (an important step).

This suggests an area the African Church could look into. The Church needs to consider what is the essence of marriage, and try to adopt a practice which will meet this, rather than allow practice to be dictated by fashion or non-essentials. It may be worth remembering that the Church used to regard a simple agreement to marry as constituting the marriage contract. The church ceremony was a solemnization, a public declaration and a blessing, but not, originally, actually essential. Since the Reformation,

---

[15] Some of these additional factors include:

(i) A minority of relatively well-off or middle-class women remain in unmarried relationships by preference because they do not want to lose their independence; they hope their partners will marry on their terms, otherwise they will defer marriage.

(ii) Some women are reluctant to marry in case their partner has concubines of whom they are unaware.

(iii) The breakup of the family unit by migrant labour has made the possibility of living unmarried more familiar. It created by force a number of female-headed households, or households in which the man was "semi-detached", and this pattern thereby became a possible option.

governments and churches have introduced restrictions, for example, states require some public record of a marriage. The Roman Catholic Church now requires members to marry in front of a priest. The Church of England does not, and will recognize any legal ceremony as a valid Christian marriage. In Scotland, marriage by mere public declaration was valid well into this century.

The missionaries, however, introduced a requirement for a church wedding, and indirectly encouraged western trappings. Partly this was out of a desire to distinguish Christian marriage, partly out of a desire to westernize. Perhaps the time has come to go back to the older Christian idea of marriage by agreement. At the least, the African Church should consider whether western trappings like the gown should be discouraged in order to make marriage affordable. Marriage is too important to be put off for a gown.

Some Concepts with Great Significance Needing Reinterpretation

Procreation

Procreation: in traditional Tswana culture, power over procreation is of vital importance. The husband pays *bogadi* to the wife's family, and thereby acquires complete ownership of the wife's procreative power and the offspring. Thus, even if the children are not biologically his, they belong to him. If the man is sterile, he may arrange a surrogate father from amongst his friends, chosen either by himself or by both him and his wife. If the woman is widowed while still of child-bearing age, the deceased husband's younger brother has a duty to procreate children by her who will be raised and considered as the children of the deceased husband. The idea is that the procreative power acquired by payment of *bogadi* should not be wasted. By the same principle, if the woman proves to be infertile, she and her family have a responsibility to provide a substitute, from among her sisters or cousins, to produce children to the husband, who will be raised by the husband and his (infertile) wife.

Consequently, Tswana girls grow up with the belief, firmly embedded both in their conscious and unconscious minds, that child-bearing is an indispensable part of womanhood. This idea is not necessarily wrong in itself, but, once taken out of its cultural context, it produces problems. Young Tswana girls, but also boys, experiment not only with sex but explicitly with fertility. The culture encourages fertility, and the original contextual constraints have gone. Thus large numbers of children, born to such young mothers, fall on the laps of the girls' families. These children are the responsibility of the girl's family, because where no *bogadi* has been paid, there is no link between the families.

Bogadi ensured that mother and children always had a place. However, despite the large numbers of children now born outside this system and its guarantees, there are very few abandoned children. This illustrates the importance given to children in Tswana culture, and also the fact that families have, to some extent, adapted to the new situation.

Absence of bogadi: a new situation.

Let us consider a few typical examples:

(1) A young unmarried girl, A, has a child, X. X becomes the responsibility of A's family. Thus both A and X are supported by the same guardian. But suppose A's mother is also a single mother, dependent on her male relatives. These relatives, perhaps one man, will become responsible for all these people, three generations or even more.

(2) In the above case, the male relative is an older man. But if A has a brother in work, he will be expected to support her and her child X.

(3) When X grows up, he will be expected to support his mother, A, and any further children she has. This is in fact very common. If one of these children he is supporting is a girl who herself has a child, he will have to support that child as well, and so the pattern repeats itself.

It is clear from all this that the extended family system is continuing to operate, and it would be quite unfair to think that the prevalence of unmarried mothers shows an abandonment of responsibility by men. As the above examples illustrate, lower-income men are often bearing very heavy responsibilities in supporting female relatives. But while they support sisters and mothers, they are not able to support their own children. Thus responsibilities have been shifted rather than abandoned. Nevertheless, this new pattern does mean that there is no longer any connection between fatherhood and responsibility, which encourages the trend of uncontrolled fertility. The new pattern is unsatisfactory. Children lack fathers. The extended family is coping with the problem, but the problem remains. Given the heavy responsibilities men are bearing for sisters and mothers, it is perhaps understandable that they are inclined to take advantage of the ability to escape responsibility for partners and their own children.

Children born outside marriage have become a familiar and accepted part of normal life. The churches, faced with a dilemma as to how to relate Christian teaching to such a situation, no longer excommunicate unmarried mothers as they once did. This acceptance of the situation applies both to main-line and some African Independent Churches, including the ZCC. The government has also accepted this pattern as normal: the standard birth-registration form no longer has a space for the father's name.

In response to this problem, Botswana law now imposes a responsibility on men who have fathered such children to pay maintenance for them. This law is of recent origin, and although maintenance is limited to P40 per month, a limit which has been criticized, the passing of this law indicates a recognition of the prevalence of the problem. However, many, perhaps most, women are unaware of their right to maintenance, and even those who are aware often consider it not worth the trouble to go to court for such a small amount, which inflation has made even less significant. And even if they do get an order for maintenance, many men succeed in avoiding payments.

The suggestion has been made that it might be more practical for maintenance to be in the form of a lump sum payment, to be invested and held in trust for the benefit of the child. Not only would this avoid the impracticality of regular payments, but it would be more in keeping with the traditional custom of paying for such 'damage' by a single payment of compensation (in cattle). It would also be a more effective deterrent to men than the present system of small and almost unenforceable payments.

Women also need, however, to take more responsibility, and to be prepared to say No. In the traditional system, the emphasis on women's reproductive power was offset by the role of the family, who enforced the marriage contract and ensured that a man who did father a child could not evade responsibility. In modern circumstances, however, these checks have been removed, and so the drive to prove fertility becomes a source of serious problems. It is also probable that the traditional attitude to fertility reflects the vast land area, relatively small population and high mortality which were the background of traditional Tswana societies. Again, the circumstances have radically changed but the attitude has not. Botswana now has a very high rate of population growth, and with a young population, in which women outnumber men, this could lead to serious overpopulation.[16]

The ideal

Formal and stable marriage remains the ideal for Tswana, yet the systems which should build it have become obstacles. Our theology should take into account tradition, culture, reason, and participation in the community. On these bases the Church needs to modify systems to make them serve the desired ends. *Bogadi* is a familiar concept with great importance in linking families. It is notable that early missionary attempts to dispense with it proved not only unfeasible but damaging. But *bogadi* can be modified. This has already begun, with furniture or cash often replacing the traditional cattle. The present day cash amount is approximately P5000, the possible price of two cattle (as *bogadi* is always paid in pairs). The essence of *bogadi* is a transaction between families; there seems no reason why the amount could not in modern circumstances be made more affordable. The sum is after all symbolic, not a woman's market value; the Church could take a lead in introducing a symbolic *bogadi* in which the emphasis is on the meaning of the transaction, not the amount, retaining the essence of the tradition.

Similarly, the Church could try to make the church wedding less of an obstacle. The question of dress is not trivial, because Tswana take great pride in good appearance, yet western gowns and suits are extremely expensive for average Tswana. Could the western trappings be replaced with African style? Admittedly, fashion is notoriously difficult to control, but at least the Church needs to recognize the problem. I am trying to identify problems, it will be up to African Churches to find the solutions in their own way. Any reformed style of marriage would probably need to be agreed between the major churches.

---

16 The national population growth rate is 3.4% per year, which is regarded quite high by global standards. Both men and women have been growing at the same rate (G.N. Lesetedi & N.L. Ngcongco, 1991, "Population and Housing Census Dissemination Seminar", 1995, p. 117).

Sexual ethics

In present day Botswana sexual activity among young people (and not only young people) seems to have become disconnected from permanent relationships. Partly this may be connected to the decoupling of fatherhood and responsibility noted above. What we see is neither traditional Tswana nor classical Christian ethics. Can the Church offer something which will help? At present, the Church is simply repeating traditional formulae which it knows no-one is listening to, and the Church no longer seems to set much store by them. It cannot go back to excommunicating unmarried mothers, nor should it, but surely it can try to say something of relevance? I do not have an easy solution here, but AIDS statistics make it obvious that there is a serious problem which cannot be ignored. The present-day West does not offer a model; its sexual ethics are clearly highly confused as well, though in different ways. The African Church needs to find African Christian solutions.

No African theology can be complete without women and there are now several networks of women theologians in Africa. The topic we have been dealing with, how the church can relate realistically to the problems that women have to deal with, such as issues of marriage, family and the status of children, etc., is one area in which the input of African women theologians is vital. These issues cannot be decided by men and imposed upon women in the church. So what is the position of women in the church? What role do they play and how are they relating to church structures, are they satisfied in the church as they find it now etc., are there some issues that cannot be left unaddressed?

Women and the Church

I now wish to look more directly at what part women play in the church. (After all, in African tradition it is the women who do the cooking.) My analysis here follows from research I did in 1990 among women in Gaborone.[17] (This is of course now six years old but there is no comparable more recent data.) There was a high rate of church membership, indicating that women were looking to the Church for something. But there was also a very high rate of turnover of membership, women moving from

17 Saroj N. Parratt, "Religious Change among Women in Urban Botswana", pp. 73-84.

one church to another; so it seems equally apparent that whatever it is they are seeking, many of them are not finding it.

The research covered three areas representing different income groups, to be representative. Gaborone women are urban now, but are mainly rural[18] in origin. Of the 1413 sampled, a mere 2.6% had been born in Gaborone, and 7.7% came from Lobatse and Kanye. 18.1% came from other places within a 50 km radius, and the rest - more than half - from further afield. Educational background, with over 35% having less than primary leavers' standard, and only 9% claimed "professional" qualifications.

Churches were classified for the purpose of this research as "main-line" and "African". Almost all the main denominations in both categories are represented in the survey: in the main-line group, UCCSA, Roman Catholic, Anglican, Lutheran, Dutch Reformed, Pentecostal, Seventh Day Adventist, and Methodist, and a few others marginally represented; and in the African group: ZCC, Spiritual Healing, Twelve Apostles, St John African Faith Mission, Head Mountain of God, St Paul, St Peter, African Faith Mission, and others marginally represented. Many of the African churches originate in South Africa.

Among the "African" churches, the Zionists are the most prominent, constituting perhaps 10% of all Christians in Botswana,[19] and 9% of my sample. The next largest in Botswana as a whole are believed to be the Spiritual Healing and Head Mountain of God Churches, although in my sample the latter ranked only seventh in size, perhaps because of its mainly Kalanga base.[20] There are a large number of small churches, some of a single congregation, accounting for 21.9% of my sample.[21] The figures are complicated by multiple membership; in particular many Tswana who belong to main-line churches also go to African Independent churches for healing, for which the main-line churches are not felt to be effective.

---

18 "Rural" in this sense includes the "traditional towns" or villages. These are now reclassified as urban.

19 Don Boschman, "Studies on the Church in Southern Africa", Vol. 3. (Departments of TRS and History Publication series, University of Botswana, Gaborone, 1994); Rachel Friesen, "A History of the Spiritual Healing Church in Botswana", MTh, Toronto School of Theology, 1990.

20 Obed Kealotswe, Doctrine and Ritual in an African Independent Church in Botswana: A Study of the Belief, Ritual and Practice of the Head Mountain of God Apostolic Church in Zion", PhD, Edinburgh, 1993.

21 These proportions are similar to those reported by James Amanze, *Botswana Handbook of Churches*, Gaborone: Pula Press, 1994.

40% of my sample identified themselves as church-goers, although only 14% did not describe themselves as Christian, and only 4% described themselves as traditionalists. (It is unclear what exactly this means, for example, when a "traditionalist" in Gaborone dies, how is she buried?) Women make up the large majority of church-goers in all denominations. Exact figures are hard to come by, but I am at present carrying out some observations at particular church services in Gaborone. At the Anglican Cathedral, 163 women[22] attended, and 97 men (two services). At the Roman Catholic Cathedral, (also two services), 411 women and 275 men. At the UCCSA, 413 women and 92 men. Apostolic Faith Mission (two services), 402 women, 203 men. I will be attending other African churches in due course.

The only exception to this pattern so far was the Open Baptist Church, with 151 women and 151 men. It may be significant that this church is almost entirely composed of European and African expatriates.

Of those who attend church, no fewer than 40.9% (231 out of 565) have changed their affiliation. This very high rate of membership turnover indicates considerable religious uncertainty. Overall the main-line churches have tended to lose members to African churches; the UCCSA suffering the heaviest losses. Although the African churches have gained numbers overall from the main-line churches, there is nevertheless a large degree of movement between different African churches, suggesting that discontent continues. Those African churches which have become more "established" are doing much less well than the newer movements; the ZCC in particular showing only a marginal overall growth.

Those in the lower income groups are more likely to change affiliation. In the richest of the three areas, only 9% changed, compared with 15% in middle-range Bontleng and 20% in Old Naledi, a poor area.

Some women had left the Church altogether. Although this was a very small proportion of the total sample (1%), it represents 6% of those who have changed affiliation.

Reasons given for changing affiliation varied. Practical reasons such as transport, or their previous denomination not having a church in Gaborone, were significant, and the largest group cited personal reasons such as join-

---

22 Youths were included in the count but not children.

ing the church of husband or parents.[23] These personal reasons are connected with Tswana women's dependent position; being expected to follow parents, husband, etc. in church affiliation. Some did not respond, and a number gave the puzzling answer "no reason".

However, the second largest reason was dissatisfaction. Variously expressed, sometimes as simply as "I lost interest". Others cited more detailed criticisms about belief and practice; some apparently trivial but in fact representing important theological or practical issues, for example covering of the head or wearing of uniforms. Covering the head is a sign of submission. Wearing of uniforms has complex associations including perhaps domestic service, especially in the South African context, and kill individuality. Thus theological issues of individual personhood may be involved. Quite apart from the symbolism, uniforms can be a heavy expense for some Tswana.

A small but important group is that of women who left main-line churches for African churches because they were denied opportunities to preach in public. This suggests that the argument that African culture is an obstacle to women's ministry may be misplaced, since it is the African churches which are allowing women's ministry and the supposedly western churches which discourage it.

Some women changed church in reaction to church discipline with which they disagreed, in particular when churches refused to baptize children born out of wedlock. Some also moved because of disagreement with church policies against drinking, though it is doubtful how strictly these rules are kept by the UCCSA.

In some cases a church was seen to have failed by not providing a sufficiently elaborate funeral service, or if members did not attend funerals in sufficient numbers; reflecting the high importance modern Tswana culture places on funerals. (In present-day Botswana funerals have in fact become bigger than ever since the funeral can be delayed while people travel from considerable distances and the service is prepared.) This is one area in which the main-line churches have an advantage, especially over the smaller African churches, being able to offer impressive liturgy and larger-scale organization.

---

23 This happens when a child has been brought up by grandparents but then rejoins the parents; a common pattern in Botswana.

Another major cause was conflict within the congregation, especially leadership struggles in smaller churches; although the main-line churches are not immune, as the fist-fights in the Ramotswa Lutheran Church illustrate.

In a few cases, women feared they were being bewitched by other members of their church. This was found both in the UCCSA and African churches. Witchcraft belief is clearly still prevalent; in the survey 95.3% believed that both witchcraft and protective measures against it were commonly practised. This suggests that the Church needs to address such concerns more directly, instead of ignoring them. The Church's tradition includes rituals, such as incense, holy water, exorcism etc., which appear to have something in common with traditional African charms, and could perhaps be part of an approach to the problem. There is a clear pastoral need here, since belief in charms is normal among Tswana Christians; it therefore falls to the theologians to find a response which is pastorally effective as well as theologically sound.

Another important reason for moving to African churches was healing (both physical and mental). Although the main-line churches have now introduced healing services, the general view is that the African churches are more effective. Even within the African sector, some are more highly-regarded than others, and members of other churches may go to the ZCC, St Paul's Apostolic, or Spiritual Healing Churches for healing.

Specific religious reasons were sometimes mentioned, such as "They have better witness". Worship with "more spirit" was desired, in contrast to the "boring" services of the main-line churches.

The apparent dissatisfaction has led to a significant drift away from organized religion altogether; more than half did not attend church regularly. The 14% who did not identify themselves as Christians may not actually be non-believers, but their response does suggest that the Church is not important to them. It is up to the Church to find out why.

The main-line churches are more popular with educated women. This may reflect these women's western education, which makes the service less unfamiliar. However, the main-line churches have undergone some Africanization, and it is possible that the association with chiefs is more important than the association with the west, which has become steadily less relevant as missionaries have departed. In other words, the main-line churches have an attraction to higher-status or better-educated Tswana as part of a local pattern, just as some churches in the west have more appeal to higher or lower status groups: a class distinction, not precisely a western/African distinction. Main-line churches cannot now be seen simply as missionary churches; they have incorporated significant African cultural elements such as greetings; ululation at weddings and baptisms, and a lengthy exchange of peace. A notable example is the practice of prayer with the bereaved. Such practices reflect the African sense of human solidarity, and are an innovation compared to the British background of the original mission churches. Many of these apparent African innovations are in fact in keeping with aspects of the New Testament which European churches have neglected. Yet in spite of all this, the main-line churches are still foreign to many Tswana women.

Conclusion

The missionaries, in seeking to establish a Christian culture among their converts assumed that their own European culture was a Christian culture, and therefore African culture should defer to it at any point of difference. Recently, however, some seem to have gone to the other extreme and assume that indigenous culture is beyond criticism and Christianity must in all cases accommodate it. What the Bengal case shows is that culture can be criticized and reformed in the light of the Gospel, but from within, keeping what is good and adapting on the basis of Christ rather than a missionary's culture.

The Bengal reformers, in acknowledging Christ, put Christ in the context of the world. They did so from a background of a literate culture and an advanced philosophy within the Hindu tradition, which made it easier to do so; they did not theologize from folk tradition. (In traditional Africa, of course, there was an oral tradition which equates to both the "high" and "popular" traditions of literate cultures.) They had accepted aspects of Christ's teachings, and had applied them, bringing transformation in society and changing the status of Hindu women. In this they established the universal position of Christ, and showed that Christ is not owned by the Church (meaning, here, especially, the Church of the missionaries). African Churches have a comparable approach, in acknowledging Jesus as a centre.

African Christians have taken some of the events of the Bible, and teachings of Jesus, as a basis in their struggle for freedom against socio-political oppression. Now, the desired freedom has been achieved in South Africa. When an African looks at the wholeness of life, this whole includes social, political, economic and religious aspects, for both women and men.

As the political goal has been achieved in South Africa, attention now shifts to the other factors which are essential to this wholeness. One such factor, which has been addressed in this paper, is the condition of women in relation to marriage, family and position in the Church. This article has concentrated on Botswana women, for whom I have specific research data, but I hope that the conclusions are of wider relevance.

If we remember that Christ is owned not by the Church but is for the world, it will be easier for African Churches to put Christ in their own cultural context. To the theologians cooking their theology in African pots, I end with two questions: "Who is Christ in this context?", and "What does Christ say in this context?"

Cook First, then Publish

Klaus Fiedler

1. Theology Cooked in an African Pot

The term "African Theology" has often been misused to denote one type of theology in Africa, which could be characterized as published, strongly influenced from the West,[1] ecumenical, conference-borne.[2] Not withstanding my esteem for the theologians mentioned, I think it is wrong for one limited group to assume or be given a name for the whole. I therefore take African theology as theology done by Africans,[3] comprising as many different theologies as there are in existence in such a large continent[4] with such a vibrant and varied church.

While defining African theology as theology done by Africans, I think that foreigners living in Africa should also be given a little room in it. Some of them, through long residence, learning and sympathy may be able to produce a theology which Africans can accept as genuinely local, and others may make a contribution as collectors, organizers or facilitators of African theology.[5] [And finally, African theology may be seen as profiting from the field of theology done in Africa.[6]]

---

1 A neighbour of mine once disparagingly called it "air-ticket theology", because much of its production depended on the availability of air-tickets to attend conferences.

2 I think many of the authors argue that they work *against* a theology that is Western influenced. But that may prove my classification.

3 These days, African is no longer a racial but a geographic term. So African theology must include, maybe in a special subsection, the theology done by the theologians who belong to the white tribes of Southern Africa.

4 This surely includes the "Black Theology" of South Africa. But it should not claim or made to be the only black theology just as much as [Ecumenical] "African Theology" is just one of many African theologies.

5 I can imagine that, for example, in writing the history of an African church, even a real foreigner can do a good job and present a fair picture which an African church *may* accept as its own.

6 Much of my argument on publishing after cooking applies equally to theology done in Africa by non-Africans.

Most of African theology - as of any theology - is oral. It is preaching, singing, praying, reading the Bible, discussing and, foremost, believing, that makes theology. The theological writers, though they can contribute something very important, should not see their limited contribution as the whole. Yes, they do make (written) theology, but it is also (oral) theology that made them.

In Africa there are millions of theologians who cook African theology, and what they cook, tasty as it is, is very varied.[7] While most of the food is still being cooked on the traditional three stones, the number of fireplaces wasting less energy and using more sophisticated equipment is growing fast. As there is nothing wrong with African theology cooked in an earthenware pot on three stones, there is equally nothing wrong with African theology cooked in a modern state-of-the-art kitchen which is equally African.[8] And while the food crops will undoubtedly be grown in Africa, I think there is nothing wrong with a few foreign spices.

That is as it should be: Cook and eat, and thank God for the food and ask Him to bless what you eat. On this wide background of theology as nurturing the Christian faith in Africa, in my article I will concentrate on a much more limited sequence: cook and publish.

When William Carey, the great Protestant pioneer missiologist, wrote his book that paved the way for the Great Century of mission,[9] he predicted that one day, if the Christians start missions among people of those remote countries, who then seemed so wild, there would be able writers who would be qualified to produce learned treaties to defend the Christian faith. Carey's prediction has long been fulfilled. The church is no longer Western/Northern as it then used to be,[10] nor are the theologians. But much of what they produce is hidden.

---

7 This is often regretted, but do you really like one-party food, and that for all of your life?

8 "African" is often being associated with traditional, rural and sometimes antiquated notions. I consider as African what is relevant for Africans (wherever it may have originated), not what has its roots in some "African past".

9 William Carey, *An Enquiry into the Obligations of Christians to Use Means for the Conversion of the Heathen*, Leicester: 1792. - The term "Great Century" was used by the mission historian Kenneth Scott Latourette to cover the period 1792-1914 during which Christian missions radically changed the religious map of the world.

10 There were Christians outside the area, for example in the Near East and in India, theologians included, even in Carey's time, and he was aware of that, but they were of a very different type of Christianity and not much missionary.

2. Publish Oral Theology

Oral theology, by its very virtue of being oral, is not published. It is very much alive, it is very effective, but its use is limited in space and time. But oral theology, if some of it is recorded and made accessible, can make a contribution beyond its important, though limited area.

First it can enrich written theology, and second it can act as a cross-check on theological ideas cooked in the kitchens of the sophisticated, rich and educated.[11] Written theology can profit from oral theology because oral theology is lived theology, a good check on what academics do.[12]

If oral theology has a role to play even beyond its original context, then it would be the task of theologians and theological institutions to "translate" some of the oral theology into written theology. This idea has been applied successfully in some cases to the study of African Instituted Churches.[13] But the method should be applied to "mission-churches" as well, since it would be wrong to assume that the oral (real!) theology is what their ancient confessions or their modern (Western) theologians may make us assume.[14]

Since scholars must be humble, they should be aware that it is not only them who can and do publish oral theology. It has gone out of fashion, even in Europe, to publish sermon collections of famous preachers, but

---

11 Research in parishes in Malawi (CCAP, Catholic, Anglican) led by Kenneth R. Ross showed that the published African christologies had little, if any, impact. What then is the real African Christology?

12 In Germany the theology taught in the universities is often seen as being detrimental to the faith, and sometimes it is indeed. The many churches in Germany with their declining membership (and often even more declining commitment) could definitely profit by paying more attention to oral theology as real and lived theology of German Christians as against the often artificial theology of the institutions training their ministers.

13 For Malawi Hilary Mijoga has done a limited survey (Hilary Mijoga, *Biblical Exegesis in African Independent Churches in Malawi*, Sources for the Study of Religion in Malawi, no. 14, 1991) and is now working on a major project, analyzing 500 fully recorded sermons. The first result is: Mijoga, H., "Hermeneutics in African Instituted Churches in Malawi," *Missionalia*, Vol. 24/3 (November 1996), pp. 358-371.

14 First attempts to do this for Malawi are: Ross, K.R., "Preaching in Mainstream Christian Churches in Malawi: A Survey and Analysis", *Journal of Religion in Africa*, Vol. XXV/1, pp. 3-24, also in Kenneth R. Ross, *Gospel Ferment in Malawi: Theological Essays*, Gweru: Mambo: 1995, pp. 81-106; Ross, Kenneth R., "Current Christological Trends in Northern Malawi", *Journal of Religion in Africa*, Vol. XXVII/2 (1997), pp. 160-76.

nowadays to publish them as tapes has become quite common.[15] Other non-academic ways to publish oral theology are the publication of "practical" Christian books of "applied" theology.

3. Publish Church History

Contrary to what some people think, I consider church history to be part of "theology proper", and one way to describe it would be to see church history as the study of the interpretation of the Bible in life.[16]

Since church history reflects God's great deeds with humankind, the record of these must be kept, and since church history reflects men's sinfulness and limitations, its study will contribute to humility, which is a high Christian virtue. Therefore, the pursuit of the study of church history can serve as a useful check on the thinking of the "theologian proper". Firstly I take an example from the North:

Logical reasoning convinces me that Calvinist theology is best, but church history tells me that Calvinists were the best evangelists and missionaries when they had absorbed enough of Arminian theology and/or practice,[17] and that effected Africa greatly.[18]

Or let me take a more recent and more directly African example. Current "African Theology" glories in telling us how the missionaries got it all wrong,[19] and when the people have heard and/or read it a hundred times, they will take it as a fact when they read it for the hundred and first time.[20] But a study of real African church history will quickly reveal that things were never that simple, and that the loud cry for "inculturation" (Catholic) or "contextualization" (Protestant) is an insufficient antidote for whatever has gone wrong in the churches in Africa.

Western theologians, equally prone to the sin of simplification, may

---

15 At least among the Charismatics. That they are, like it or not, on the cutting edge of Christianity in Africa, cannot be denied.

16 CLAIM intended to do this for Malawi, but after doing a little it concentrated on selling foreign books in Malawi: There are plans to reestablish its publication arm.

17 A case of Calvinist theology coupled with Arminian practice is that of Charles Huddon Spurgeon, the famous preacher and great supporter of the faith missions in Africa.

18 The Dutch Reformed Missionary movement, which affected countries like Malawi (Nkhoma Synod) and Zimbabwe, was strongly influenced by Arminian concepts.

19 Even in evangelical circles this is quite *à la mode*.

20 Repetition of opinions is a powerful theological argument.

admire and glorify everything in African Christianity, from the East African Revival ("Continuing powerfully for more than 50 years!") to Ujamaa ("isn't that the real embodiment of the spirit of the Christian gospel?"). The study of African church history could help them to cut down on wishful thinking[21] and to learn to see where God's Glory really is in Africa.[22]

Church history needs to be studied, and that will help those who do it to become wiser (usually). But it must be published, if many are to become wiser. Take the example of research which has remained unpublished for too long.

Isabel Apawo Phiri studied the religion of women among the Chewa from pre-Christian times up to the present.[23] She found out that in early Chewa society women often had leading religious roles,[24] and that missionary Christianity deprived them of such leadership. But in other ways that same mission Christianity empowered Christian women in many ways.[25] This was strongly promoted by South African single and married women missionaries, who in 1940 set up Chigwirizano as the women's own organisation, and it became a powerful organization for fellowship, service and evangelism.[26] When the missionary women had handed over leadership of Chigwirizano to Malawian women, things changed. Women were considered to be too immature to lead and organize themselves and the Synod (not the conservative missionaries from that apartheid country) decided that women can never meet, except in the presence of a respected man, the "sitter-in-between" (*mkhalapakati*).[27] This says a lot about the official theology of Nkhoma Synod of the Church of Central Africa Presbyterian

---

21 There are also methods to study African Church history as a field for the projection of one's own concepts. An example from Germany is: Jürgen Günther, *Mission im kolonialen Kontext. Beiträge zur Geschichte der Mission der deutschen Baptisten in Kamerun 1891 - 1914*, Initiative Schalom, 1991, 148 pp. [MA Hamburg 1985].

22 A German professor ended his article on Christianity in Africa with the statement that "African Christians are increasingly less interested in denominations". This says much about the author and nearly nothing about Africa.

23 Written as a PhD thesis for Cape Town University, published as Isabel Apawo Phiri, *Women, Presbyterianism and Patriarchy: Religious Experience of Chewa Women in Central Malawi*, Blantyre: CLAIM, 1997 (Kachere Monograph no. 4).

24 *Ibid.*, pp. 23ff.

25 *Ibid.*, p. 11.

26 *Ibid.*, p. 71ff.

27 *Ibid.*, pp. 87-90.

(CCAP). Women can not be leaders, not even lead women. And from observation one can learn even more: The "sitter-in-between" is not to be the women's leader, but when I saw the various groups of chigwirizano women come to the funeral of the mother of a friend of mine, it was always the man who led each group, not at the top, but just in front beside the top.

I think this study of church history (including Church history as recent as a few days ago) needs to be published. The *mkhàlapakati* is a real theological innovation, cooked in an African pot, quite unique, though admittedly not of my taste.

4. Publish Written Theology

The publication of African Church history is not only needed to build knowledge, academic and otherwise, but it is perhaps even more important for the building up of identity, and in this case it is the identity of African churches that needs to be defined and enhanced.[28] If African churches define and develop their identities, that will be a good base for theological work in various areas, besides church history.

Much writing in African theology never gets published. For some writing that is definitely the best solution, but for others it is a pity. Much good quality material is indeed hidden, maybe in the writer's desk or in a more or less obscure library.[29] Therefore my demand: get the texts out of their hiding places, make them public, and that is still being done these days by printing books.

Publication is not only a means to spread information, it is also a means to improve information. As long as something is written for internal use, or even as a dissertation, usually less care is applied and less rigidity. Therefore, if for all writing the aim of publication is kept closely in view, the writing itself will profit from it. The aim is not to publish whatever is being written, but to write whatever is being written in such a way that it can be published, and then carry it through and do publish it.

---

28 In many cases it may not be a big difference if such writing of church history is done by a member of such a church, by an African from outside that church or by a foreigner living there, as long as the church can identify with that written history.

29 A library, especially of a University, is a public place. The very important dissertation by Andrew C. Ross on Blantyre Mission was available for four years in Chancellor College Library as a microfilm copy. I know of one person who used it in four years.

In order to achieve this it is important to aim at a change of mind: We have learnt now that black is beautiful. The next step is to learn that local is good. Theology can and should be cooked in a local pot, theological training can be done locally up to the highest level, and theology done locally should be published locally. This new mindset is different from the prevalent one that everything really good can only be from abroad. If you have that mindset, your work will conform to it.

If we want to publish African theology, it should be done locally. Publication abroad is not intrinsically wrong, but usually the books published in the North are expensive, rare and difficult to come by in Africa, and in some cases publishers of dissertations in the North know little quality control.[30] So while occasionally an African book should be published (or co-published) in the North, local publication should be the normal thing. Otherwise local products will always be dispised.

The aim must not be simply to publish a good book, but to establish theological publishing in Africa countries. Therefore the task of the theologian in Africa is not just to think, teach, write, and publish, but also to sell. Books sold will enable new books to be written and new thinking to be made, while books sitting idle on a shelf unsold will bind precious capital and discourage publication, research, writing and even thinking.[31]

Kachere Series: one way to do it

Our experience shows that theological publication is possible in Africa even in a poor country like Malawi: Up to 1995 hardly any book in academic theology was published in Malawi, though the Department of Theology and Religious Studies had been publishing an annual journal[32] and editing a simply produced series *Sources for the Study of Religion in Malawi*.[33] In 1994 we decided to establish our own publication arm, and

---

30 A remarkable example for this is Harvey Sindima, *The Legacy of Scottish Missionaries in Malawi*, Lewiston/Lampeter/Queenston: The Edwin Mellen Press, 1992, a book filled with hundreds of mistakes. Mellen Press never responded when I inquired. The book has 152 pages, and we bought it for £36.95.

31 In the North, academic publication, especially of monographs, is not possible without sibsidies. This option should not be completely excluded in Africa. In Europe and America though, subsidies are usually very high. Publishing in Africa can be cheaper, therefore in many cases subsidy by love and labour is sufficient and no cash subsidy needed.

32 *Religion in Malawi*, edited by Joseph C. Chakanza, started 1987.

33 Altogether 17 brochures were published.

we called it *The Kachere Series*, using as our logo the wild fig tree, under whose shade people would meet, be it for conversation, court cases, or religious activities.[34]

The aim was to produce books which pay their way, but we subsidize them by our love and labour. We do all the work from the manuscript to the camera-ready copy. Then the books are published by either Mambo Press, Gweru, Zimbabwe[35] or (mostly) by CLAIM, Blantyre.[36] For three books we received the money to print them from the Association of German Protestant Churches and Missions (EMW), to start a revolving fund. The idea worked, up to now 20 books have been made and payed for, and there is money for another four or five books, and sales are continuing.

The Kachere Series shows that it is possible to publish books locally in Africa, and surely it is not the only possibility. This approach has its limitations in that the time available to the members of the Department as editors of the Kachere Series is, of necessity, limited. In planning for publication all emphasis should be put on doing it. There are many obstacles, and usually there is no chance if one waits for the great, good and impressive solution.

Create a market

The theologian's task is not just to think, teach, write and publish, but also to sell, because only books sold are an encouragement to make more books.[37] In selling African books, information is a problem. Therefore each publisher (and ultimately each writer) should establish a sales network. The channels used for this should be low cost, so advertising is usually ruled out. But mail is usually cheap and so is labour to write addresses. An upcoming possibility may be e-mail and ultimately the inter-

34 Chief Kapeni of Blantyre, who welcomed the Church of Scotland missionaries in 1876, had many Kachere trees, David Livingstone met the chiefs of Nkhotakota under a Kachere tree. Leornard Kamunga, Malawi's first saint, as a missionary in Zambia build his church beside a big Kachere tree, and even Kamuzu Banda, Malawi's dictator of so many years, learned the alphabet in amission school under a Kachere tree (but we do not blame the tree for that).

35 This is the case with the Kachere Books. We had hoped that publishing with an established publishing house would increase sales. Print runs are about 1500.

36 This applies to Kachere Texts and Kachere Monographs. Their printruns are 500 or more, smaller printruns and shorter distances make the management easier.

37 This is a valid reason for small printruns. Higher printruns do not make books much cheaper, but books sitting on shelves unsold tie up capital and discourage writing.

net.[38] Book reviews in relevant journals are another way of advertising books, but this process is always slow. Another important element in selling books are personal contacts. When you go to a conference, go and sell books, as well. There are people who are willing to buy!

A new and highly recommendable attempt to gather and spread information about African theological books are the *BookNotes for Africa* published jointly by the Theological College of Central Africa, Ndola, and the Harare Theological College.[39] Another venue to explore is the annual Zimbabwe Book Fair in Harare, where we expect the Kachere Series to be represented in 1998.

One of the perennial problems of African theology is the scarcity of money. But money there is, local and foreign, and some of it can and must be used to buy African books. Maybe here as well, a change of mind is necessary!

Creating a market is not only selling books, but also creating the demand for them and maybe even producing them, according to demand. When books are used in courses, students may buy them, and books written by their own lecturers are an attraction for students.

Once books are made in Africa, they should also be sold in the North, and since there is more money over there, prices can be put up a bit. There are a number of libraries which are happy to establish a standing order for all books, and there are other interested individuals and institutions. It is worth the effort to try to find them.

One possibility is to find a sales representative maybe in America,[40] Scotland[41] or Germany.[42] Other possibilities include direct mailing, representatives at conferences, book reviews in relevant journals.

---

38 Up to now we have sold a few books via e-mail, and we have created our first Kachere e-mail flyer. A well wisher put the Kachere books on a page in the Nyasa Net discussion group on the internet, which also brought in some orders.

39 The first appeared 1996, biannual subscription is $6 within Africa. One issue may contain around 40, one paragraph book reviews, for books from "obscure" publishers addresses are included (BookNotes for Africa, POB 250100, Ndola, Zambia).

40 In America our sales representative is International Scholars Publications, Dr Robert West, 7831 Woodmont Ave 345, Bethesda, MD 20814 USA, austinispl@aol.com. From there the internet bookshops like amazon.com are also supplied.

41 Here the Church of Scotland, Department of World Mission, promotes and sells our books noncommercially because of its historic interest in Malawi.

42 In Germany all our books are copublished by Culture and Science Publ., Friedrichstr. 138, D 53111 Bonn. This puts them on the European book data bases, but sales up to now are small.

Create a critical reception of African theology.

All theology being produced should be available for and open to critical reviews and thereby provide building bricks for further theological developments. Critical reception may start with books reviews in theological journals, but perhaps the most important critical reception takes place in academic teaching.[43]

Further reception may take place in academic dissertations which in turn may and should be published,[44] so that African theologians are not just studied outside Africa, but that dialogue between them increases.

Non African themes

I think that African theologians are normally expected to write on "African" topics. Why? Are they not theologians, and is not the whole field of theology open to them? Why should Africans always write about Africa? Why not write straight-forward dogmatics? And if Africans write it, there will also be room for African or local perspectives wherever appropriate. I know that "Africanness" increases market chances, but a market, locally and internationally, should equally be sought or established for "non-African" themes.[45]

5. Degrees, Publications and African Theologies

Everywhere in the world dissertations are a major source of theological production.[46] Small wonder, since it takes usually two to four years full-time just to write one. By definition a thesis is to be a contribution to knowledge,[47] and therefore each doctoral thesis written by an African should push African theology at least one step forward.

---

43 Here care should be taken that courses on African theology do not just take one section of the theological spectrum instead of the whole.

44 One case study is Augustine Musopole, *Being Human in Africa: Toward an African Christian Anthropology*, New York et al: Peter Lang, 1994. It is a pity that, being published in the USA, the book both required a sizable subsidy *and* sells at a high price (more than $40).

45 We thought that Hilary Mijoga's dissertation should be published as a book not in the Kachere Series, but in a specialized series for New Testament studies (with International Scholars Publications) so as to feed it into the academic dialogue on this subject. But it still is African theology.

46 And this applies even if one takes into account that dissertations everywhere differ in quality.

47 This is fully true for doctoral theses, but, depending on the university or theological institution, for a Masters thesis often "an orderly statement of the existing knowledge" is acceptable.

What William Carey predicted in 1792, has come true, Africans are producing "well-conducted treatises in defence of the truth".[48] But I am astonished that these many dissertation seem not to have pushed African theology forward by very much. Why?

1. It seems to me that the majority of dissertations remains unpublished. For some theses this is definitely the best solution, but for many others it is a pity: So many years of work (and a lot of money), so much effort, a real contribution to knowledge and all that in three copies in an obscure library![49]
2. Dissertations that are published are mostly published outside Africa, and because in the "developed" world the salaries are also highly developed, printing monographs over there is very expensive.[50] Usually high subsides are required,[51] and even after the subsidy has been paid, the prices of the books do not match African incomes.

Africa has not only the disadvantage of low wages, but also the advantage. And since offset printing has done away with the typesetting (even in Africa not cheap), and since computers and laser printers are now more easily available in Africa, it is quite possible to publish monographs with no subsidy except in love and labour.[52] A bit of innovation is needed, but theologians should be happy to be innovative. That they are conservative and never come up with anything new, is just a myth.

Publication is the acid test for a dissertation

If a dissertation is a contribution to knowledge, this contribution must be

---

48 The first doctoral dissertation written by a Malawian may be this: Harry Chikuse, "The Validity of Banthu Marriage", D.D., Theological Faculty of the Pontifical Urban Athenaeum of the Propagation of the Faith, Rome, 1944.

49 My PhD dissertation may serve as an example. Written in English for Dar es Salaam University, a copy was duly deposited in the Library. Over 20 years I have heard of one person who ever used it, while its German translation sold 800 copies. But for Africa the dissertation and thereby the results of serious research practically did not exist. To make up for it, the English version was finally published: *Christianity and African Culture: Conservative German Protestant Missionaries in Tanzania, 1900-1940*, Leiden: Brill, 1996, printrun 600.

50 In Europe few monographs are published without a subsidy. The printruns are between 200 and 800; they would be commercially viable with printruns of 3000.

51 A German mission publisher offers to make an average length dissertation with a printrun of 200 for a subsidy of 4000 DM. Other publishers demand twice as much for a printrun of maybe 300.

52 In some cases it may be wise to try to co-publish with a non-African publisher, matching low African wages with a developed sales system in Europe.

published. Therefore write a dissertation always with the book in view![53] If that rule would be followed, the quality of dissertation would improve. So many dissertations contain little of anything new and are filled with review and repetition of what others have done and published before. To know the material that others have produced is a prerequisite for a thesis, but that is background and has no room in the dissertation itself. This, surely, does not exclude an introductory chapter, but if four of six chapters are such, that is simply too much, and (non) publication shows it.

To me it seems that supervisors often have strange ideas and low expectations. Why should every dissertation on Malawi start with good old David Livingstone, then tell us about the early missionaries, detail the problem of the church under colonial rule and then proceed to tell us how we finally realized that Kamuzu Banda was a bad dictator and then that the Catholic Bishops finally started the dismantling of the dictatorship with their Lenten Pastoral letter of 1992. Why? We know all that, why repeat it instead of doing research and producing something more limited, but new? There are such big gaps in research. Why not start filling them instead of rehashing what others did before and usually did much better?

To write in view of publication will also encourage students and supervisors to take more care of the technical aspects of a dissertation: style, format, spelling, the cutting out of redundancies, proper arrangements of sections, footnotes, tables and bibliographies.[54] I know it is a big thing to get a dissertation finished and that they are hardly ever perfect, but to keep publication constantly in view would make everything more realistic and act as quality control.

Research on lower academic level and publication

What fascinated me when I was a student in Kampala at Makerere College of the University of East Africa was that even first year students were encouraged to do research. During my three years at the Baptist Theological College in Hamburg I had not learnt this. The many opportunities Africa offers for primary research should be utilized to the full. One can

[53] I still remember vividly, when my first supervisor, Dr Louise Pirouet, told me, "Klaus, you write a dissertation, but mind you, in reality you are writing a book".

[54] It is painful to read external examiners' reports that speak of careless preparation, bad style, tables and captions being mismatched, and then include 2 pages of mistakes to be corrected. That was the work of the student and of the supervisor to check!

indeed expect first year students to make a contribution to knowledge, though their research is unlikely to produce the big book right away. But care should be taken to preserve whatever is collected and make it accessible for further research, and some of it, in one way or another, should find its way into publication, as a research contribution, as an article in a local journal, may be as a booklet. A good Bachelor's dissertation may even form the basis for a booklet. In addition publication in non-printed form may be considered.

In order to make most of the many small dissertations being written for Diploma or Bachelor, an early look at possible publication would be helpful. It would help to avoid topics that are too broad and where the student can neither contribute anything new or precise. The aim is not to publish everything written, but to write in such a way that much can be published in one form or another.[55]

Degree work abroad

Most African degree work is still done outside the continent. This looks strange to me, but both sides like it: International students bring in high fees, and they look good on a promotional leaflet, and to work for a degree oversees does not only widen the horizon but also improve the personal economic situation. All very good reasons, but why should academic Africa export her best resources, the students?

Of the postgraduate work done abroad, some is good, very good or excellent and should urgently be published. But much postgraduate work done overseas is simply not publishable, because of a wrong degree design. It is normally expected that "internationals", to use the American term, write about their own country. Then they are expected to introduce the country, its history etc. Finally there is a bit of research, usually at the very end. And then they take the dissertation back to Malawi and are surprised that its arrival creates very limited excitement. But then, why should it? There is little new in the dissertation, and the supervisor should have thought of that in good time. Had the supervisor thought of a possible publication, the dissertation would have been much better, and it would have made a real contribution to knowledge.

---

55 Bunda College of Agriculture of the University of Malawi now requires that every MA candidate produce, besides the dissertation, at least one scientific article for publication.

I think that it is a wrong approach that an African student should invariably write about her or his own country, even in such remote places as St Louis, Mississippi, with no chance of primary research. Why should she or he not do real solid research on St Louis or on any area that can be reached easily from there? Or, turning the argument around: why should a student who wants to write about Christian - Bahai relation in Zimbabwe do that in Germany and not in Harare? And after having done good research, detailed and rich in data, why not publish it with Mambo Press in Gweru?

6. Publish in All Media

I have so far concentrated on publishing in book form, and for a long time to come I expect the book to be the most important medium for publishing. Still, other methods should be explored.

Journals: Compared to books, journals are more flexible, and therefore can take up recent research results more easily. There should be many theological journals on various levels in Africa. This is not so difficult if you keep the committee level low and the commitment level of one or two individuals high.[56] The key is to do the manageable, and not to hesitate doing it.

CD ROM: A CD ROM disk can accommodate the content of a small library, and they are not expensive to make. Since a CD ROM disk can take so much, it seems to me to be the ideal medium for publishing the big amounts of information that have been published already (and sold out), that are published in obscure journals and/or have never been published. A CD ROM can easily take material that would not warrant a 500 print run, but which nevertheless contains valuable, primary information. The CD ROM supersedes the microfilm,[57] being cheaper and more versatile, since one can copy files from it into an ordinary computer and since a CD ROM drive is much cheaper and much easier to handle than a microfilm reader.

Electronic Publishing: This is still a largely unexplored medium, based on the internet. The concept is not to print the text, but to keep it (for 25 years or so) on a server, so that everyone who visits that website and wants

[56] Also in publishing books, committees, especially international ones, seem to be a very effective way of delaying things.

[57] An excellent example for the use of this now outdated technology is the collection on New Religious Movements by CENERM, Selly Oaks.

a copy, can download it to her or his computer and make a printout.[58]

Print on Demand: This has been applied to dissertations very effectively by University Microfilm International in Ann Arbor, MI. The concept is easy: UMI makes a microfilm of a dissertation, and the customers can - on demand - get a bound printout on any of the many thousands dissertation available. The system is cheap to the authors, so African dissertations which for one reason or another are not to be printed, should be offered to UMI.[59]

But the principle which UMI employs can also be utilized in Africa, adapted to changed circumstances. The idea would be to store the texts not on microfilm but on computers.[60] They should be properly formatted for A5 and then, when a customer asks for it, a printout would be made and properly bound.[61]

8. Economic Considerations

Africa is famous for its poverty, and as much as lamenting about it is justified, it does not help, and poverty is a very useful argument to construct a vicious circle or two: "Africa is poor, therefore we can not publish books, and even if we publish them there would be too few people to buy them. So there is no need to publish books in Africa." Or what about this: "Since so little is published in Africa, that little can not be taken seriously. So there is no point of publishing in Africa at all. We'll wait for an offer from Azunguland. And if that does not come along, it is their fault."

Poverty is Africa's disadvantage, but there are advantages, too: labour costs (and that includes printing) are low, and postage is low.[62] African publishing can profit from this situation, turning round at least one disadvantage.

---

58 Some of the classic texts of world literature are already available on the internet in scholarly editions. Why not put African texts there? There may yet be few capable servers in Africa, but the internet is expanding rapidly.

59 University Microfilm International, 300 North Zeeb Rd, Ann Arbor, MI 48106, USA.

60 ZIP-Disks, taking 100 Megabytes, would be a good choice for storing much.

61 For smaller pieces, A4 could also be considered, but for books only A5, so that it can join other books on a decent shelf.

62 Postage in Germany has become so high that the *Magazine Evangelikale Missiologie*, which I edited for 12 years, was later printed in and posted from Bulgaria.

European academic publishing, especially of monographs, is highly dependent on cash subsidies. If African publishing is well organised, less or even no subsidy is required, at least as long as much of the editorial work is done by the authors, their friends and maybe a few lecturers of theology.[63]

What makes publishing expensive are overheads, wages and books unsold. Much theological publishing can be done as a spare time activity of the theologians, or of the authors. This reduces the wage bill. Many theological institutions have a shelf which is not yet full, and that can accommodate the stock of books. And if the print runs are low, books will not remain unsold for too long.[64]

To get started, an occasional investment or a little subsidy from abroad may be a good idea, and support of this type is available. But African publishing, though it can profit from a little overseas support, must not become dependent on it, its structure must be basically self-supporting in order to be viable over the years.

9. Publish

Africa is a continent full of Christian theology. Most of it is talked, prayed and sung. More should be written, much more, and then, publish, do not hesitate.

---

63 Kachere Monographs, printrun 700, require no *cash* subsidy, but we are glad if some of the authors or their friends can afford to buy, right at the start, 50 or 100 copies.

64 Offset printing makes it possible to have low printruns *and* to keep a book on the market for a long time, since the plates of the first printrun (of maybe 500) can be preserved, and thereafter even reprints of 100 are economically viable.

Member Institutions

Africa University, Faculty of Theology, Mutare, Zimbabwe
Baptist Seminary, Gweru, Zimbabwe
Chishawasha Major Seminary, Harare, Zimbabwe
Gaul House, Harare, Zimbabwe
Kgolagano College, Gaborone, Botswana
Mindolo Ecumenical Centre, Kitwe, Zambia
Morija Theological Seminary, Lesotho
Murray Theological College, Masvingo, Zimbabwe
Nazarene Theological College, Lilongwe, Malawi
Seminario Maior De S. Agostinho, Maputo, Mozambique
St Anthony's Major Seminary, Kachebere, Malawi
St Augustine Seminary, Roma, Lesotho
St Dominic's Seminary, Lusaka, Zambia
St Peter's Major Seminary, Zomba, Malawi
St Pius X Major Seminary, Maputo, Mozambique
Theological College of Zimbabwe, Bulawayo, Zimbabwe
The Regional Seminary, Chishawasha, Zimbabwe
United Methodist Theological School, Cambine, Mozambique
United Seminary of Ricatla, Maputo, Mozambique
United Theological College, Harare, Zimbabwe
University of Botswana Dept of Theology and RS
University of Malawi Dept of Theology and RS
University of Swaziland Dept of Theology and RS
University of Zimbabwe Dept of RS, Classics and Philosophy
Zomba Theological College, Zomba, Malawi

Executive Committee Members

Published by:
ATISCA,
c/o Rev. Dr. N.O. Keolotswe (Secretary),
Department of Theology and Religious Studies,
University of Botswana,
Private Bag 0022, Gaborone, Botswana

Correspondence to:
Dr. Klaus Fiedler
Editor, ATISCA Bulletin,
Chancellor College,
P.O.Box 1037, Zomba,
Malawi

www.ingramcontent.com/pod-product-compliance
Lightning Source LLC
Chambersburg PA
CBHW021908020426
42334CB00013B/513
* 9 7 8 9 9 9 0 8 1 6 6 5 5 *